Praise for Joan Williams

"Death of a Salesman—Southern Style"

"*Old Powder Man* begins like any of a hundred drearily competent novels. . . . But there is one difference between *Old Powder Man* and the hundred other novels; those novels are forgotten in a week and this one is memorable. It is memorable for the basic quality that lifted Joan Williams' first book, *The Morning and the Evening*, from the ruck–a simple and natural instinct for the moments of human feeling. Like a water-witch, Joan Williams can walk over the most unpromising territory, and suddenly her willow wand bends toward the spot where the living spring lies hidden.

. . . .

Old Powder Man might, however, almost be called a novel of anti-technique. But what in the beginning may seem a clumsy veracity emerges in the end with the dignity of a method. It is as if Joan Williams had said, 'Life isn't all a matter of focus, it's a matter of mist and drifting too, not a matter of controlled meanings but of a sudden, stumbled-on vision, and this is the only way for me to tell the truth about it.' It is a dangerous game she is playing, but the feeling redeems all.

My second observation has to do with the way Miss Williams regards her world. This is a Southern world, a part of the world immortalized by Wolfe, Welty, McCullers, Faulkner, Katherine Anne Porter, Flannery O'Connor and Tennessee Williams. Irreconcilable differences are of course to be found among these writers, but there is one quality they all share–the need to seek intensifications, to lift life, to twist it, to shake it as a terrier shakes a rat, to make it reveal something beyond itself. Joan Williams asks only that it reveal itself." —Robert Penn Warren, *Life* magazine

"There's Power in Powder Man"

"What is unexpectedly fine is the fullness of a strongly male character, among chiefly male contemporaries, and the convincing details of a dynamite salesman's life blasting levees up and down the Mississippi River. . . . The result is a full portrait of a strong-willed man in a tough struggle for success, almost a 'man's book' if the term were not so irritating and the novel too good to be hemmed in by artificial categories." —Doris Betts, *The News and Observer* (Raleigh)

ALSO BY JOAN WILLIAMS

The Morning and the Evening
Old Powder Man
The Wintering
County Woman
Pariah and Other Stories
Pay the Piper

Remembering

Remembering

Joan Williams' Uncollected Pieces

Edited by Lisa C. Hickman

The stories and essays in this book previously have been published and are reprinted here with permission: "Remembering," *Ironwood* 17 (Spring 1981); "Scoot," *Key West Review* 3.1 & 2 (Fall and Winter 1989) and Rpt. *Southern Reader* 3.2 (September/October 1991); *Seymour Lawrence Publisher: An Independent Imprint Dedicated to Excellence.* 25th Anniversary 1965–1990. Seymour Lawrence, Inc. 1990. "Celebration," *The Double Dealer* 1.1 (Fall 1993); "The Contest," *The Chattahoochee Review* 15.4 (Summer 1995); "Happy Anniversary," *The Southern Review* 31.4 (Autumn 1995).

Cover photograph of Joan Williams by William Leaptrott,

Courtesy Peggy Leaptrott

Cover design by Mauricio Díaz

ISBN: 978-1-5040-2876-9

Distributed in 2015 by Open Road Distribution
345 Hudson Street
New York, NY 10014
www.openroadmedia.com

For my honeys, Jeffrey and Jordan

And my mother,
Patricia Louise Arch

Contents

Introduction

Collecting the last of Joan Williams' scattered short stories and non-fiction pieces feels like engaging in an ongoing conversation with her. They appeared in the final two decades of her life—a sometimes difficult and tumultuous period with a second divorce and the death of her companion, Seymour Lawrence—and the themes she selected for the stories resonate with maturity and gentle humor. There is no disputing the skill, agility, and emotional wallop of her prose, though she would say, "No one is interested in my quiet little stories."

I met Joan in the summer of 1993 while working on a *Memphis* magazine article about William Faulkner and the two Memphis psychiatrists who treated him in the early 1950s. At the time she was living with publisher Seymour Lawrence in a house mere blocks from Faulkner's home, Rowan Oak. The house had been an impulsive purchase by Seymour, or Sam, as Joan called him. He woke her one morning in their hotel room in Oxford, Mississippi, and told her, "I've bought a house. And it's across the street from Rowan Oak!"

Apparently for Joan there was no escaping Faulkner. He is credited with influencing her first short story, "Rain Later," winner of the college fiction award for *Mademoiselle* and an honorable mention in *Best*

American Short Stories 1949, though the story's publication *predated* her introduction to Faulkner. And she took enormous pride when, thirty-four years after its publication, she recalled that "'Rain Later' stood up on its hind legs" and was included in her lone short story collection, *Pariah and Other Stories*.

But *Remembering* is not about William Faulkner and Joan Williams. That story has been told. *Remembering* is a celebration and recognition of a remarkable writer who dedicated more than fifty years of her life to a craft she considered "a life's process that entailed a lonesomeness of spirit."

A silent terror stalks the wife in "The Contest," a story Joan published in 1995, nine years before her own death in 2004 at seventy-five years of age. A couple married fifty-five years banters about attending an upcoming fair hosted by their small, rural community that offers a number of contests, including a dance contest. The story, told from Mary Virginia's viewpoint, is a brilliant back-and-forth of past memories converging with present events to force fearful clarities.

Mary Virginia's story is consumed with the faults and infirmities of her husband, Aaron—his hearing loss, failing eyesight, bad driving, skin so "thin and pale, he appeared luminescent," and his small feet and shoes "no bigger than an elf's"—while unbeknownst to her, he is enjoying a renascence of sorts. In her mind's eye, she regards herself as being in much better mental and physical shape than her spouse, even as nagging doubts nudge closer to the surface. The shock of Aaron, whom she considers "a bag of bones; a sick old man," winning the dance contest with another woman, "a woman he's took up with," intensifies her emotional fragility and unraveling. The palpable terror she feels as her mental state collapses and she seeks refuge in their walk-in closet culminates in her recapturing the lines of Fats Waller's song, "Your Feets Too Big."

The upbeat title of "Happy Anniversary," also published in 1995, belies the reality of a couple facing a fiftieth anniversary party with trepidation. As the husband, Tate, anticipates this auspicious event, he concludes he was rushed into an early marriage because of the war, " . . . now he felt he ought to shout out to somebody, Watch out, Brother!"

A degree of ambivalence and bemusement colors how the couple appraises their long union, and the narrative moves them closer to a future centered more on endings than beginnings.

At seventy-five years, the husband and wife are dealing with various health afflictions that introduce a sense of despondency and loss of control. "He is tired of replacing the old with the new, clogged arteries with cleaned-out ones, a true heart with one of plastic, a hip of bone with one of metal. Nothing seemed real anymore. Sometimes at night, he thought he heard Allie's new hip clanking beside him. Before she got it, the old one sounded like it needed oil."

The success of both stories is attributable in no small part to Joan's seasoned approach. She manages to capture both the friction and rewards of marriages that span decades, and illustrates it in "Happy Anniversary" with a simple reflection: "He could never let himself be caught malingering, standing empty-handed, because under such circumstances Allie always looked at him queerly, asking, What are you doing Tate? He never found the voice to answer, Thinking, woman."

In "Scoot," which appeared in the *Key West Review* in 1989 and was reprinted in the *Southern Reader* in 1991, Joan again highlights mid-to-late-life concerns. This time, the eponymous central character, Scoot, is a hard-working, older African-American woman who cleans hotel rooms for a living and continues to support or help support a number of her children. Her life has been difficult: married at twelve years of age, mother to seven children, abandoned by her husband and struggling financially. Two of Scoot's sons are in prison, and she continues to worry about them and what their future may or may not hold. "She had no idea what Hootchie-boy would do when he eventually came out. She was tired by now of his even calling up collect. I'm tired of other folks' mess, tired of chillens, and tired now of their chillens too, she could think."

Contemporary elements of the story merge with the rural setting, poverty, and black dialects. The men in the penitentiary are giving themselves permanents, wearing gold chains, and "getting sissy." Unemployment, layoffs, government housing, and work programs receive brief mentions. Inside the homes the "black and white shadows of television jumping everywhere." Her own grandchildren require renaming. "She had given all her grandbabies different names, because she could hardly pronounce or spell any of the ones they had. When Little Sister and Lean were in the hospital having them, she had cried out, 'Where you get all these names!' And they had calmly answered, 'Off television. Out of magazines.'"

The central action of the story involves a cosmetics party hosted by one of Scoot's daughters. The woman selling the cosmetics is white, and Scoot reluctantly agrees to try the moisturizer. Relaxing under the woman's application, Scoot's thoughts turn again to her exhaustion; her boredom with her job; and the stress of her living conditions.

Throughout the story, the images of wind-blown objects, of a sense of floating or flying, are maintained. The first paragraph of the story ends with Scoot thinking of herself as a bird: "Bending and swooping sheets over beds all day gave her the sensation of being a half-flying bird." And later, at the cosmetics party, feeling " . . . bad and out of place. She wished she had not come; and like the moths that had flown in, folding wings and settling into a dark place between the refrigerator and a wall, like a tiny alleyway, she took a chair there and settled down too."

Being stationary fills Scoot with a sense of sadness. "At the corner church lot, she turned home, where several cars were still mired down after the last Sunday's rain; some of them were already missing hubcaps. She could feel a certain kind of sorrow about those stuck things; they seemed so silent and waiting, like they would never move again: until maybe Judgment Day when everything got weighed."

In the end, Scoot chooses motion. She chooses to do something for herself. She will change jobs, move, and dismantle her home that is a revolving door of children and grandchildren. Yet, her resilient spirit and loving attitude disallow a complete separation: "All she knew was if your chillens didn't leave you, you had to quit them. And it was time. She couldn't help but smile, either, thinking how any road she went on would never have a lonesome end to it, with all those people she had coming along behind."

Nonfiction is a genre Joan frequented with rarity, though she was perfectly adept at its demands. In 1992, she wrote a feature story for *Southern Accents* magazine about Faulkner's residence in New Orleans during his very early career, "Sanctuary of the Storyteller." She was a contributor to a book of essays by Seymour Lawrence's authors, friends, and family. And over the years she gave a number of speeches and remarks, one of which, "Celebration," appears here.

Her essay, "Remembering" (1981), however, represents the greatest departure, and for that reason and others, it is singular in its appeal.

To celebrate twenty-five years in the business and his independent imprint, Lawrence published *Seymour Lawrence Publisher: An Independent Imprint Dedicated to Excellence*. This book appeared in 1990, six years after Joan and Lawrence rekindled their friendship in 1984. Joan and Lawrence lived together until his death in 1994.

Apparently Joan's submission to the anniversary book and Jane Turnbull's, proprietor of the Turnbull Literary Agency, were among the last to arrive. Their names were penciled in on the contributors page. The slender, ninety-five page volume featured notes of appreciation and admiration from fifty-two contributors. Many of Lawrence's authors such as Jim Harrison, Richard Yates, Rick Bass, Tim O'Brien, William Humphrey, Thomas McGuane, Tillie Olsen, and Kurt Vonnegut participated; as well as his children, Nick Lawrence and Macy Lawrence Ratliff; and Oxford, Mississippi, bookstore co-owner, Richard Howorth.

Joan's brief note includes a handwritten aside at the end in which she addresses Lawrence as "Fluff," and a reminiscence of the lunch date when she introduced Lawrence, who at the time was an editor with *The Atlantic Monthly*, to Faulkner. Lawrence pitched a story idea to Faulkner, and the author responded with such alacrity, that Harold Ober, Faulkner's "amazed" agent, asked, "What did you do, Mr. Lawrence?" Faulkner's "A Note on Sherwood Anderson"—sparked by his lunch conversation with Lawrence—appeared on the cover of *The Atlantic Monthly* in June 1953.

The occasion that inspired "Celebration" was the second annual meeting of the Pirate's Alley Faulkner Society in New Orleans. The September 1991 event coincided with Faulkner and Joan's side-by-side birthdays, his September 25 and Joan's September 26.

Joan's address recalls Faulkner's anguish about what, if any, legacy he would leave. "I remember one time his quiet look of inner dejection and despair—and I regret I can't remember what words led up to his saying, 'With the mark I seem to be about to leave on this world.' Meaning, at the time, he seemed not to be about to leave any mark at all."

But more cheerfully, Joan also remembers Faulkner's appreciation for life's happier moments. "He loved the celebration of birthdays. Mine is the day after his and through all the years, he never forgot. A telegram always arrived: 'Many happy returns on your birthday and love.'"

Three years after Arkansas poet Frank Stanford committed suicide in 1978 by shooting himself in the heart with a twenty-two caliber handgun, Joan published "Remembering." Stanford was on the brink of a literary breakthrough, having released a year earlier a 15,283-line poem and co-founding Lost Roads Press. A bit of a cult figure, Stanford's popularity remains today. Lucinda Williams, singer, songwriter, and friend of the poet, included "Pineola," a song about Stanford and his death on her 1992 album, *Sweet Old World*.

Joan first heard of Stanford when he was a baby. Stanford's adoptive father, Albert Franklin Stanford, known to her as "Mister Frank," was a friend of her father's, P. H. Williams. Stanford was an engineer who helped her father build the levee system along the Mississippi River in the Mid-South. Joan was a frequent guest at the Stanford home in the Arkansas Ozarks.

Joan's essay finds its way among many threads that lead to discoveries about Stanford as well as herself. When years later Stanford sent her some poems with an inscription across the top—*You never knew I was in the next room writing too*—she realizes with some surprise that she was a role model for the young man. She recalls Stanford from infancy until his final, very encouraging visit with her in the early 1970s—"And I see him moving about as if he needed exertion to tell me the final summation about his life: everything was going well and far better than he could ever have dreamed. When he left I was filled with so much happiness, thinking how far he had come"—then not so many years later there is the devastating letter from his mother with an obituary enclosed.

"Remembering" discusses the role of guilt, so prevalent with any death, but especially a suicide. Joan worries she should have done more for Frank when he shared his work with her, "Had he, in sending me poems and a short story over the years, been asking something which I in my replies did not give? . . . Though, finally, absolving myself of guilt, and no longer even asking why, I only hope Frank found what he wanted. And maybe that was not even peace, but who he was. At last."

Joan fretted—perhaps more so in later life—over her divorce from her sons' father, Ezra Bowen, and the impact of that separation. Frank's death triggered remorse about the breakup and deepened her awareness of Dorothy Stanford's sorrow. "Long afterward Dorothy would cry in her mother's anguish, 'Oh, didn't he know when he killed himself he killed me too!'"

Grief, guilt, and loss, feelings very few people escape knowing, find expression near the essay's conclusion: "In back, there was a patio where Dorothy and I often sat alone in the evenings. . . . It was a pleasant time for the adults, when everyone was fed and the house settled. On a wall in my house now there is a picture taken on that patio. Two small brothers have their arms about one another and are smiling and holding up fishing rods. Behind them the lake is so intensely blue it seems to be dancing, despite having been stilled permanently in the sunlight by the camera. Ill winds had not yet blown in to touch us. The little boys had no idea that within a few years their parents would divorce rather unthinkingly: lives gone atilt would never right themselves in the same way again."

It seems only fitting that this new book shares the title of Joan's Frank Stanford remembrance. For friends and admirers already familiar with Joan Williams, *Remembering* is a wonderful opportunity to revisit this author; and in turn, it may serve as an introduction of sorts to a new generation of readers.

—Lisa C. Hickman
Memphis, Tennessee
September 2015

For more information about Joan Williams see *The Mississippi Writers Page* and *William Faulkner and Joan Williams: The Romance of Two Writers* (McFarland).

Remembering

FICTION

Scoot

All that morning she had the strange feeling something would happen. Scoot cleaned up her assigned rooms at the motel as soon as possible. Bending and swooping sheets over beds all day gave her the sensation of being a half-flying bird.

Later on, she drove the distance across town to Midnight's Grocery to pick up things needed at her house. On that stretch of road, the few stores on both sides with flat roofs looked smaller. They seemed to her like people with hands on their heads trying to keep trouble off. Scoot wanted to laugh. Black clouds rose and fell, leaves blew turnabout, signboards bent. She wondered if the day was giving her an uneasy sense.

After she let shut the grocery's screen door, some boys who were lined up by the gas pumps turned her direction. "How you doing, Scoot?" She did not want to answer. "All right." Then one boy wanted to know, "How A.Z.?" She told him, "Hootchie-boy doing all right." She knew what was coming next. "How Will?" She shot back another answer. "Will doing all right." She drove away with those boys in the rearview mirror, drinking and drugging, jiggling change in their pockets, loose-jointed as clothes hanging on a line. *Huh*, she thought.

A woman with two sons in the pen gets their respect. She believed those boys were headed the same direction, living off the state. As hard as she worked, that got her goat.

Scoot turned off old 51 at a stoplight and headed home a few short blocks. In the distance, across a railroad that was noticeable if the sun was just right, shining like spittle, was the road newest to these parts, the super. Everything was happening its way. A shopping center was built out there and land was being cleared for the first hospital in the county. Out there was the Quality Rest Motel. From inside, Scoot stood listening to the roar of the semis passing and to the frizzy-whizzy muffled sounds of cars speeding past.

On her side of town, she went by Head Start with its yard full of oaks and bare of grass. This close to her house was another place those boys without jobs hung out when the school day was over. It was here Hootchie-boy broke in. He had been home on parole and ought to have had more sense. "All he had did was end up with mo'time in the pen. Time on and on," Scoot said. "Me and my other chillens have hardly knowed him." She meant Hesther, Brother, Lean and Little Sister. Hootchie-boy had gone to the pen at eighteen and now he was a man nearing thirty. She could hardly remember a time when she didn't have to go down to the Delta on visiting Sunday twice a month. "Down in the Delta in the summertime the musquitoes could tote you off," Scoot said. "Heat can fry your brains limp. Good gracious!" She had no idea what Hootchie-boy would do when he eventually came out: She was tired of other folks' mess, tired of chillens, and tired now of their chillens too, she could think.

Because that had been the second time Hootchie-boy messed up on parole. The first time he robbed the very grocery she had just left, Midnight's. No wonder those boys stood there smirking, she thought. She never would figure out what Hootchie-boy had thought he'd get out of that man's register, little as he sold, nothing but piddling stuff. It was a waste. And every time she thought about the police coming to her house that night, she shivered again. They had been so polite. "Where's A.Z., Louise?" they asked. The police always knew when Hootchie-boy was at home because a sergeant at Parchman prison called up and told them. So, when a store was robbed in his neighborhood, they naturally came to see where Hootchie-boy was. That stormy night when she heard a knock on her house, Scoot flew out of bed. Rain had swept all inside when she opened the door. "He in yonder in bed, sleep," Scoot answered.

Hootchie-boy was there too. The police brushed past an old half-raggedy curtain left up in that house when Scoot rented it, which separated a bedroom from the kitchen. She could see that curtain moving inside her head yet, moving in hindsight. Hootchie-boy had raised up out of the bed. Only his clothes lay over a chair sopping wet, and beneath the bed were what he called only his 'tennis,' side by side. She could see those two shoes yet too, and their dark tracks leading from the window to the bed.

In time, her son Will went the same direction. Will was the baby; and he went on down to the pen after Hootchie-boy. It was then Scoot had a feeling the whole pattern of it had been laid out before she was born, and they were born either. All the roads she drove these days seemed to go whish to the Delta no matter the direction she was driving. Sometimes Will was in trouble when she got to the pen. The trouble he got into, he had always gotten into the same way. "Will was always following along after the other fellow, doing what somebody else had said did," Scoot said. "One night some boys came by the house asking, would Will hep them tote a safe? He went on with them. Will thought they meant tote it from one side of a room to the other. He hadn't knowed they meant tote it out of the Chevrolet place."

At a corner church lot, she turned home, where several cars were still mired down after the last Sunday's rain; some of them were already missing hubcaps. She could feel a certain kind of sorrow about those stuck things; they seemed so silent and waiting, like they would never move again: until maybe Judgment Day when everything got weighed. Along her road some houses of her neighbors were almost hidden, they had so many green plants. Some hung at the end of ropes, some were caught up by chains, and others sprang up out of flower beds. She missed having a garden, but working, she had no time to fool with one and nobody who wanted to help her. Back out in the country where she had lived in another lifetime, married to Lish and having babies, she grew everything. Back then, she had married Lish when she was twelve-years-old. "And thought I had did something," Scoot said. But he never messed with her till she was ready. "At foteen," Lish said. Her hair had been down to her waist, and Scoot hadn't even known how to comb it. Lish's mama fixed it; they lived with her. Lish would say how he let Scoot go on to school. Afternoons, she cut out paper dolls from magazines with Lish's niece. At Christmastime, Lish's mama gave her Santa Claus along with the rest of the kids. Then finally she and Lish did go to bed. "And up stepped Little Sister," Scoot said. She did not even know what had happened. Lish's mama had to tell her she was pregnant. Then she got mad and told Scoot she was a "fast heifer" and ought to be home with her own mama looking after her.

When she turned on to her road, Scoot could see all the flowers she did plant these days, just some cock's comb, red and fancy and fuzzy, to keep herself reminded about the ground and growing.

She had no place to park except on the road, then she cut down steps over a culvert to her house at the bottom of a hollow. To her, it was like something hunkered down there. She was afraid when there were heavy rains because then the ditch filled, and she was always afraid some of the little children playing around there would fall in, drown, and get swept off this earth. She did not know where all that water went. When Scoot tried to imagine, she pictured up the highway to Memphis, but then the pictures stopped. Around there where she was born and grew up was all she knew about. But Lish had tried being on a government program one time and was sent up to Michigan to lay pipe. "That man seed a bear!" Scoot liked to tell.

Her daughter Lean and her two children lived with her. At the house then, (and they were there a lot,) were Little Sister's little children, playing, because Little Sister had to clean up her house. Always people were there who were not doing much to help out. Brother also lived at home and worked. But he didn't bring home nare sack of groceries, Scoot noted. And when he did buy some, he carried them over to the girl he had his babies by. Scoot had told him then to go ahead and stay on over yonder with her. But Brother always came back, keeping his little stuff back of the curtain, the way Hootchie-boy had.

If the house emptied then, like Hootchie-boy being gone, and then Will, it started filling up again, the way Lean had come back with her two children. There was no one but C. who helped her with groceries. C. had started being Scoot's boyfriend, and she wasn't certain yet how far things would go. She called him, "Old pants leg", with affection. He talked about buying her an air-conditioner when he didn't even stay at the house. C. was better to her than any man ever had been. And she didn't care a minute if he couldn't write his name, or that he didn't know it when he saw it writ, she said. Their best times they went out to the auction barn on Friday nights. At first, she had been scared. But then she learned to jump up and holler and wave like the best bidders. In fact, some nights C. had to hold her in her chair, or she'd buy too much. Her favorite thing was in the house now, a framed dog with yellow eyes that glowed in the dark. The first night they saw it, Lean's little children ran under the bed. That tickled Scoot to death. "Them chillens was scared," she said. C. deserved better than the wife he had who threw her garbage out the window. Scoot hadn't believed him till she drove out to the country where they lived, to peek, and saw his nasty yard.

Little Sister's little girl called out, "Hey, Big Momma," and Scoot told her, "Hey." The girl's name was Genevieve but Scoot called her Boo-Gal. She had given all her grandbabies different names because she could hardly pronounce or spell any of the ones they had. When Little Sister and Lean were in the hospital having them, she had cried out, "Where you get all these names!" And they had calmly answered, "Off television. Out of magazines."

Between the two sides of green duplex there was a wedge of porch. Standing there, Scoot could see in to the other renter, Miss Edna. It seemed inside her house evening had come on in, with black and white shadows of television jumping everywhere. Scoot stood there and looked back up to the road a minute. The black clouds were no longer so dark. They had separated. They reminded her of the waters in the Bible that had parted and people had walked all in between them, a miracle. Above the road sprinkles of sunshine were dancing and lighter places shone in the clouds like ribs of rope, or rows in a field, or grooves in a garden where you walked and leaves slapped you like hands. She turned back to Miss Edna saying, "The monkeys are jumping."

Miss Edna looked out. "Child, they is," she said. Scoot had known the old woman would remember too the way it used to was, she thought, back out in the fields when the sun was so hot things shone in your eyes—monkeys jumping, they were called. One of the field hands was bound to call that out, folks would laugh, and go on picking. Back then her daddy was alive. His voice would come to her over the rows as warm and soft as a quilt laid over her winter nights when icicles hung off the eaves. Her mother Rachel had seemed to be a tall woman back then, and now she was gnarled. Rachel used to like to sit down in the fields, and she would relate the white man told her, "I ain't never seed nobody sit on they butt and pick as much cotton as Rachel." That old woman's done a heap of work in her time, Scoot had said. And back then, they had kept the walls of their cabins plastered with newspapers to keep out cold; looking up at them was when she commenced to read, Scoot said.

Miss Edna was holding something in her lap, her hands kneading over it. Scoot heard ting and pling and knew peas or beans, shelled, were falling back into her bowl. There was such a slow sound to them, and she thought again about Rachel and Miss Edna waiting out their days. Miss Edna cut eyes her direction. "Singing at the church this evening," she said. "Was wanting to go to it."

Singing at the church, Scoot thought; and rafters rang above her head. But she had to tell Miss Edna with the same sense of sorrowful spirit, "Little Sister having a party this evening, and I got to go to it." It seemed then for a minute she could smell kerosene lamps from the old days, lamp wick, and see church windows shining high with their light from a distance coming along some dark country road. Back then people would hear that singing, and they'd hurry. Today, when they got to church didn't seem so much to matter. "Maybe tomorrow evening," Miss Edna said.

Scoot turned without a promise. Inside her house, Lean was holding Tamiko between her legs. "What you doing to Kat?" Scoot said.

"Trying to comb her head," Lean said. "But she holler."

"Then I'm going to do it tomorrow," Scoot warned.

"Go to church with Miss Edna and you be hollering," Lean grinned at her. She had a deep-sounding voice like Lish's, and both of them reminded Scoot of a freight train passing in the night and blowing its whistle. "I don't sit on the side of the church with them old women! They shout you out of the place."

Scoot carried her groceries to the kitchen. Hesther was dancing in to it from out of the bathroom. She was wearing a blouse you could nearly see through and drinking out of a pin bottle. "Gimme some please," Lean said. Hesther danced her direction wearing what Scoot had been told were ballet slippers, and she wondered what it was that called for flat black shoes with no arch support and elastic cutting over the instep. "Don't take much," Hesther said. "Brandy's too high."

Scoot told her, "Hesther, you going to end up just like Lil is." She meant her dark sister that stayed drunk in the road. "That woman stay drunk," Scoot said. "Lil be staggering down the road and her boyfriend no older than her son be coming along butting her rear with the front end of his car. I know I'd be picking up something and breaking that windshield."

"Maybe she getting some kind of enjoyment," said Hesther, shrugging.

"She get drunk with her son. I didn't know a mother was supposed to drink with her own son." Scoot looked at them in wonder, but no one objected.

"I'm not going to be like no Lil," Hesther said.

"You don't know. Lil didn't go to be like no Lil one time neither. She had pretty hair and that boy's pulled out chunks of it. He's bunged up on her face just because Lil went and got her period." Hesther took another sip, and Scoot wondered, *Why can't Luther do nothing with her?* They were supposed to be married; but it was possible Hesther bought her own self the little ring she wore with its stone, and Scoot went on thinking how Little Sister was buying her own self a government project house and didn't want to be married to the boy she'd been living with so long.

Luther might be her son-in-law, but all she knew was, he and she had hardly said a word to one another. She believed that boy might be so quiet because he had been to college. Luther wore a red jacket with white letters on back: NWJC. Hesther told her they stood for Northwest Mississippi Junior College. She did know that Luther's people looked down on Hesther and hers. She'd told the girl, "Let them peoples go on an stay where they stay at with they little stuff, and I'll stay with mine."

"What time Little Sister's party is? she asked.

"Eight," Lean said.

"That eight fast time or slow time?" Scoot said.

"Ain't no fast time, slow time!" Lean hollered.

"The time change and it just is," said Hesther, softer.

Scoot turned her back and looked out the kitchen window. She saw a grey and white cat walking the back fence. Its feets sharp, she thought. One of them went daintily ahead of the other one. The cat reminded her of folks on TV walking a tightrope, teetering and tottering, till you didn't know if they'd make it or not. She would hold her breath. At the window she comforted herself with the thought, if the party was at eight fast time, then it really was at seven.

Behind her, Lean was a tall thin drink of water, and dark like Lish too. Hesther was more the way she was, short and bright-colored. One time she heard a white man call her "a pretty little ginger-colored Negro." Hesther was a girl then, and she had her by the hand and hurried her on by fast. Today, she guessed she could say something back to him, but what? *Time change and it just is*, Hesther had said; and Scoot wondered what she was doing about it all. She was tired of lying those sheets through air, making neat corners, she knew that much. She bent to the screen door's bottom half, looking at Boo-Gal outside playing. Soon the girl saw her and came her direction. "What kind of party your momma having?" Scoot whispered.

Boo-Gal knew what secrets called for. She made a little fist and blew through that funnel. "Facial party, Big Momma," she said. Her breath blew through the screen door over Scoot with the same warm feel, the same smell, as a puppy's breath, like gravy. Then she darted off, her face reflecting wonder. She had seen what she never had before: Big Momma didn't know what she was talking about. Scoot stood up with her knees making cricking sounds. "You getting to be just like Grandma Rachel," Lean said.

"I ain't big as Muh is!" Scoot said.

"You getting there," Lean said.

Scoot took up a pair of pliers on the sink and started wrenching a faucet. "Man own this house ought to come see 'bout his old leaky sink," she cried out, and threw the pliers down. "He don't never come round here less it's after his money."

"He's gone to Panama," Lean said, in her deep voice. "He don't never do nothing but go to Panama to see his son."

Harmony was in the house the next minute. "What do clouds look like?" Hesther wondered.

"Can you walk around? Do it go fast?" Lean asked.

"I expect you'd have to put me in Pampers if you put me on a plane, I'd be so scared," Scoot said.

Then the minute passed. All the little children started hollering, "Luther's on the road!" Hesther ran with them, Kat still with her hair not combed right. Climbing into the big blue Cadillac, Scoot tried remembering how Luther had bought it, second, third or fourth hand? They shot on past neighbors out watering their plants who were watching and pretending they weren't. Scoot waved driving past. To a lot of them, she had said, "That car just guzzle up gas," and was proud of that fact.

Up in the front seat was Little Sister's little boy Frederic Darryl, who Scoot called Britchie-man. And in the back with her was Lean's pudgy child Cederic Levonteau. Scoot took that opportunity to remind him, "Takey, this not stopping on no highway for you some candy," so he'd set up his little howling for Lean to deal with. First, Scoot told him, "Hush up, with yo' knotty head o' hair."

"I'm going to give him a Kiddie Kurl," Lean said. "Straighten it out." That's what Hootchie-boy give hisself even if it was for kids."

"Man in the pen give himself a permanent." Luther spoke about that.

"Mens down there think mo' about their heads than I'm is," Scoot said. "Wear all these gold chains. Mens gettin' sissy. Be fixin' they faces next." She turned her own worried one to the window. "Got to put something on my face tonight and wear it a week when I got to work tomorrow?"

"A week?" Lean said. "Where you get that at? You can wash everything off tonight." Hesther turned and looked back.

"I didn't know," Scoot said. By then they were out on the highway and passing Midnight's with its lights gone out and the gas pumps dark. At that hour those boys had moved along the road to where the whiskey store shed its puddle of light. The county had only recently gone wet. Baptists had asked the new owner to put up curtains over his window so no one could look in to bottles from the road. That made the black people laugh who had worked for some of them, drinking in private, meeting a bootlegger in the woods or hauling stuff from Memphis, talking two-faced, Scoot felt. The children were cutting up all over the car till Hesther said something so quiet, they hushed. "Luther been laid off," she said.

"Is?" Scoot stared on out the window.

"Man where he work laid off a bunch of folks. Said times are bad."

"I know that's a fact," Scoot said.

"We're going to move back down to the country," Hesther said. "Live in a trailer park. I've put down a thousand dollars on one. Luther thinks Memphis is too dangerous anyhow."

How close would the trailer park be? Scoot wondered. "It's dangerous in the country now," she told them. "Nothing's the way it were." She saw relief in the glass's reflection when Hesther said, "He's picked up some carpentry work."

Scoot spoke to the back of Luther's neck. "Man got a profession he can carry with him is lucky." She thought back to the time when Lish couldn't make it on that government program and she realized then he'd never do anything again once he couldn't walk behind a plow looking at the rear end of a mule. After that he'd gone off and left her too. She knew the two things were connected. Still, she had satisfaction to this day that she hadn't taken him back when he came home sick; only Little Sister would have him. "He my daddy," she had said. And Scoot told her there was no way in the world anybody could argue with her about that.

Little Sister's house seemed peaceful from the road, till the children started in. Luther wouldn't come inside to any party just for women. When he drove off, Scoot could tell Hesther, "Don't nobody but you sign for that trailer. Sign a paper with a man and you don't know what you going to end up with." At least Hesther nodded. Little Sister met them at the door with her face so worried her freckles stood out. "I invited everybody on the block and nobody have came," she said.

"They'll be here," Scoot said. "Maybe they on slow time.

"Ain't nobody on slow time but you," Lean growled.

"Colored peoples always be slow." Lish sat up laughing in the lunge chair where he was always sleeping. That day, he'd been over to Oxford on the dialysis machine and was always worse-off and crazier-acting then. "One of yawl fix me some coffee," he said.

Scoot going by had a hard time remembering they'd ever lay down together, much less had seven babies. But sometimes, like then, when Lish was there she couldn't help remembering that boy who vanished. In Little Sister's living room there rose to her senses the old smell of hot dry pepper grass and the summer day Lil's child Boo-Boo came running to her across a pasture crying out, "June Bug's went down in the pool!" Scoot hollered and fell out, she said. The day she had told him, "You come back here, you better bring sunshine with you." But June Bug never made it home again that day before dark, he never made it home again at all.

Everybody stood shooing the children out of the kitchen, trying to eat up Little Sister's food. Looking at it set out on a pretty yellow cloth, Scoot hoped Little Sister hadn't had to lay out for all that herself. She knew she was supposed to buy something that evening to help her out. Her pay check was stretched as it was. Noting Little Sister's stomach, she had told her, "I think you mo' pregnant than you think you is." And Little Sister said, "You may be right. I know my back killing me sitting over sewing at that factory all day."

Soon the white woman she expected was there; the children all went to the bedroom with television. "This is Verna," Little Sister said. "This my family. Nobody else have come."

"They'll be here," Verna told her. Scoot said, "That's what I said." Verna carried a plastic case on into the kitchen and began setting up her things out of it. There were mirrors and trays with sunken places which she filled up out of jars and bottles. Verna's hair was piled into a cone shape and was sprayed and blond, and in the kitchen light it shone all sugary like cotton candy spun at a fair. Her husband worked at the same factory where Little Sister sewed, and was the reason she'd asked her to hold the party. Whatever way things went, Little Sister got a necklace set to keep, and Scoot was glad about that. "I axe one of yawl to fix me some coffee and not a one of yawl have did nothing," Lish called.

Finally the girls were coming in from off the block, holding open the door and letting in bugs from off the porch light. Scoot saw they were all Little Sister's age, and even being her mother, she felt bad and out of place. She wished she had not come; and like the moths that had flown in, folding wings and settling into a dark place between the refrigerator and a wall, like a tiney alleyway, she took a chair there and settled down too. Verna was telling them, "First, you'll have a mask. It'll tighten and harden, so don't worry." The girls began smearing their faces with a white cream; then Verna got out a big book with a pink cover and began reading. It was all about how her company got started, she said. "Our founder worked in a laboratory and one day looking under a microscope, she-," and Scoot wondered why in the world she didn't realize not a girl was listening.

Pretty soon Takey ran in after potato chips calling, "You all look like clowns." Lish sat up chuckling. "Look like white peoples," he said. Afterwards, there was a commotion and it was Lean jumping up, holding her throat, crying, "I can't breathe." When she ran out to the bathroom, Verna called, "Wash gently." The other girls cleaned their faces with cotton and lotion, then Verna came over to Scoot on soft footsteps and said to her, "Won't you join us?"

Scoot shook her head. Verna went on off. And shortly, when Lean's shadow crossed by where she sat, Scoot leaned out and told her, "Girl, you was scared." But Lean never looked her direction.

Verna next directed them to try moisturizer. While she talked about it, and the girls dotted their faces, she went behind each one of them and set her thumbs on their temples; she massaged round in circles a long while. The girls closed their eyes and leaned their heads backwards till they met Verna's belt buckle. Several of them dropped their mouths open. Scoot thought maybe she slept because suddenly there was Verna beside her again. "Would you like to try this?" she said.

"What that stuff is?" Scoot said. "It's for wrinkles," Verna said. And

Scoot said, "Those girls don't have any." The other older woman looked back at her for a minute. "They will though, won't they?" she said. And then she added, "It prevents them."

"That stuff's all for courting folks," Scoot said. "I'm too old." Verna went away again, and this time she handed out to everyone small pads and pencils. "I'll have to take them back up again," she said. "Please just sign your names and check off answers to questions."

The room began to have a buzzing sound like a wasp's nest being upset; buzz buzz; they asked one another questions. "Is my nose oily or dry? My eyelids crepey?" Then there she was again standing at Scoot's little cubicle. "Would you like to-," Verna started.

Scoot folded her arms, and said, "I can't read."

Verna didn't move. She stared a moment at the wall behind Scoot's head, then off another direction into the kitchen itself. Her throat worked as if there were things to be said she couldn't say: as if there was too much, dating from a long way back. Her blue eyes grew paler. In a moment, she walked off. Lean from nearby looked in at her. "How come you told the woman a story like that?"

"I'm not studying her mess," Scoot said.

Verna was holding up to the light two different bottles; for a moment then too, she looked embarrassed about what she would say. Then she plunged ahead. "I have here tonight only two shades of foundation. That's all you'd need. One for darker skin, one for lighter. Cinnamon and Honey Tan."

Lish had gone into the kitchen to make himself some coffee. He turned there in the kitchen light and said, "MY gret-grandmomma were cinnamon-colored. She were a mixed-up Indian lady. But my gret-grandpaw, he was a black African. My gret-grandmomma she remembered that Titanic going down with all them rich peoples. She remembered Abraham Lincoln slipping round in disguise to see how do the white treat the colored, wearing raggedy clothes. He freed all of us too. It's all writ up in a book."

"Daddy," said Little Sister, "Your water's boiling."

Lish came on out of the kitchen carrying his cup of coffee. The girls stood and milled around the table looking into boxes of make-up; and they began to help one another draw on faces; they put on rouge, lipstick, eyeliner, and when everyone had a cherry-colored eye shadow, they'd all begun to favor one another. In the midst of their all being busy, Scoot suddenly got up. She went out to the table and sat down.

"I'll try the moisturizer," she said.

Verna came directly over to where she was. She poured into Scoot's hand cool drops she spread over her face; then her eyes were closed and she felt Verna's fingers on her tracing lines on her forehead, rubbing her temples. She felt the hardness of Verna's belt buckle on the back of her head. While she closed her eyes, she was careful not to open her mouth, and sit there looking as if she knew nothing. When Verna had stopped, Scoot opened her eyes. It was time to buy something, and she met her own reflection in a tiny box of brushes. Picking up a fine pointed one, she said, "How much this thang is?"

"Nine-fifty," Verna told her.

"Oo-wee. For this little-bitty brush?"

"It's made of camel's hair," Verna said.

"I don't care who it made of," Scoot said, putting it back down. Another girl said, "All this stuff high. Is it as good as Estee Lauder?"

Somebody laughed. "You been watching television." Verna said, "I think it's as good." She took out her own pad and pencil. "Would anyone like to place an order?" she said.

A large girl picked her glasses up off the table, put them on and said, "I don't get paid till Friday. And that's all spent." Another thin little girl followed her out. "I don't have any money," she said. After a time, Verna said "You can place orders tonight and pick them up at Sarah's on Friday, after you're paid." Then she whispered low to Little Sister, "Don't give any girl her order till you've got her money." I'm glad the woman's got that much sense, Scoot said to herself. She went on around the table and picked herself out a lipstick. Hesther had laid out money, and Lean was giving something from her little welfare check. Little Sister wore the new necklace. Some of the girls paid cash, mostly they place orders. The children were all crowding the doorway and calling, "Luther's on the road." Hesther looked at herself once a mirror, said, "Ain't I'm cute?" and danced his direction.

But when they joined her at the car, she was pouting. "Luther says for me to wash my face," she said.

"He may be right," Scoot said, getting in. "I know you're going to have to take my face like it is."

"That woman's stuff was too high," Lean said.

"I know one thing," Scoot said. "Most of those girls aren't going to come back for what they ordered. They were just embarrassed in front of those girls who paid cash."

She felt sorry for Verna, being out there with them anyway. She supposed like most of those girls, she was earning the living these days and some man was living off her.

Lean's little children had nestled against her. Little Sister's would be asleep back in their own beds. Scoot could not help a lot of nightimes but think about Hootchie-boy and Will sleeping where they were, with all those men. But she never had slept in a house alone, and she'd been thinking maybe at her age she ought to start. She had told Brother and Lean one time they could have that house, and she'd move off to her own place. They had told her, Naw, you ain't. You'd be scared. But she was not. Tonight, when she had her eyes shut and that woman's fingers made her relax, the could see inside herself, into the dark behind her eyelids. She knew she was tired of coming out from her bath every night and finding Brother and Lean had beat her to the door. You too old. You stay home, they'd say. Tomorrow evening, she decided she'd take her clothes over to Muh's, and change at her house. Then she'd drive by and if Lean was on the porch with her hair curled, her make-up on, waiting for her to babysit, she'd been and drive right past. Lean would be so mad. She'd go on to the cafe in town. And soon she'd have her little stuff in a U-haul and she'd go off down the road to where a new government project apartment house was just opening up. Quick Chicken was always hiring, and she'd like a change. She'd like standing behind a counter and waiting on people who'd come in being polite. C. would come on when he wanted, keep her company. Maybe in time they'd get divorces and marry. If she wanted to end up taking care of a pants leg again, she thought. All she knew was if your chillens didn't leave you, you had to quit them. And it was time. She couldn't help but smile, either, thinking how any road she went on would never have a lonesome end to it, with all those people she had coming along behind.

The Contest

All that week the Abbots held friendly Mr. and Mrs. spats about whether they were going. Finally, Aaron said, "The fair's the only time the Masons raise money for that old lodge of theirs."

"I know that," Mary Virginia said. "I reckon I've been to every one they've had." Born and bred here, she did not have to tell him, he was too. "I remember the first one riding on Daddy's shoulders and looking all around."

"I'm married to an old woman."

She turned, thinking he was joking, and meant to make a smart remark back, something better than That's the pot calling the kettle black, when she saw Aaron was not trying to be funny. He sat, bending the flowered chintz spread he said was too fussy, hands clasped between his knees as if congratulating himself about something and she could ask What?—his puckered mouth turned up.

Nerve; talk about it. He was a cadaver sitting there, daring to dream. Who would want a sick old man? Silver strands of hair blew over his head every time he spoke, dancing there as thin as thread. "Uuf," he went after almost every word. "Uuf," she repeated with a wicked glance. Aaron was too out of things to notice.

Mary Virginia turned to the walk-in closet, deciding what to wear if she went, and she would have to go. Aaron could not be turned loose in a crowd alone. He would be disoriented, lost. Clothes in the hot closet were shrouds, loose-limbed. She picked at them, thinking there was always a middle-aged widow or divorcée looking for another man to ease the loneliness these women talked about. She would cater to another man the way she had the one she married, and be driven nuts all over again. Mary Virginia, having been spared that, grinned. She ruled the roost, she thought. *But Aaron?*

In her day you ought to get married and teaching was the only job a woman should have. Anything else and people felt sorry for you. Poor girl. Your husband couldn't support you. Here she sat, settled in Itna Homa all these years with Aaron. Today not married, in that other time, she might have done something. Though what, frankly, Mary Virginia could not imagine and tapped a foot, considering.

She might have developed her singing beyond the Baptist choir, or played the piano longer, stronger, harder, or taken up tap dance lessons. *Lord-a-mercy, that was it!* Her fingers flew independently to her face and her nose itched. Too late, she saw herself in sequins and snappy, white shoes. Move over, Eleanor Powell, she thought.

Heat at the lodge would be a killer even if it was late October. Dust would cover anything she wore. Hands out, Mary Virginia flipped through clothes. String from the bare-bulb light overhead scrabbled across her face and scared the fool out of her like the running feet of mice. She snatched on the light flooding herself and the floor with warm yellow. Her hands, arms and face were so covered with brown spots and freckles, she ought to stop worrying, so intermingled you could not tell one from another, which were age spots and which came from her redhead's complexion. Scared the fool out of her, Mary Virginia thought, when she already saw shrouds and now tentacles, with the arms of clothes hanging out. She chose a navy blue pants suit with sleeves, thinking it was slimming.

Who she looked after yea these many years was the bag of bones beyond. Aaron was the living dead, his pizzazz all gone. If he ever had any? If he sat fifty-five years later, like a bump on a pickle, dreaming of younger women, let him. The idea of his tottering down an aisle was funny, except it was ludicrous. Infidelity was not part of country folks like themselves. That belonged in picture shows, books, and now on TV in your own living room. She expected to look up any minute and see the act completed before her eyes. Soap opera folks were the world's worst, the limit, and she could not think what else to call them.

Standing bared, Mary Virginia remembered the pants suit as being wide-legged but hopped from foot to foot trying to wiggle it on. She had not gained all that much weight. Her stomach gurgled with Slim-Fast, the reason you lost on the stuff being it gave you diarrhea. Every morning she checked Aaron's stool for blood since he started having colon trouble. Aaron Mortimer could not do a single thing for himself and never had been able to. She had always been his mother and men grew worse about that as they grew older. Doctor their colds, sew their buttons on, everything but wipe their bottoms and that was next, she guessed.

Aaron's skin was so thin and pale, he appeared luminescent—she believed that was the word, having learned it from a friend doing a crossword puzzle. Mary Virginia's upper plate clicked in satisfaction over knowing a word not common to country people. Lit-up, lustrous, like nacre, she recalled from another puzzle; Aaron was like polished marble. Trying out words and knowledge, she thought she ought to be a writer. She longed to see her name in print one time before being in an obituary. Obit, she recalled from television. To write for the county paper, she would have a by-line and was proud of knowing that too.

Aaron sat as if posing to be an angel when she could not remember the name of a single, famous angel painting reproduced on Christmas cards every year. Veins stood out on his forehead already sunk in like a skeleton's. He never ate enough, was picky as a bird, she told him. Aaron Mortimer were the two worst names in history and stuck together like that seemed a punishment. His mother may have been suffering child-birth pangs when she named him. Mary Virginia, glimpsing herself in the mirror beyond his head, thought, Cheeks like withered apples, words learned long ago in a storybook. She knew now, unfortunately, what that writer meant. She stretched her face into a Chinaman's leer, thinking how wrinkles could go up and disappear. She longed to have her face lifted like famous people. Even Roseanne Barr looked better when you would think nothing could help that woman: scratched her crotch in public. As an American flag appeared to her mind's eye, Mary Virginia saluted: up and over quick before Aaron caught her out. Roseanne's incident happened in a baseball stadium, opening game. The "Star-Spangled Banner" played in her head and hearing, Mary Virginia wanted to be patriotic, to do something for her country, to just do—well, something, she guessed, dropping her hand back.

She put on a new white blouse with a ruffled neck. The glossy material having covered buttons gave her a sense of importance, like being an executive. She wielded an imaginary gavel, letting her soul cry out, Here, here, to gain her some attention. If Aaron sat thinking about romance, she tried recalling it in their beginning. *Shoot fire. That was the trouble with age. You forgot.* One memory surfaced of Aaron in bell-bottoms their first evening, buying her a rose on the way to his naval station in Pensacola, wearing the stupid, round hat gobs had to wear. The vendor was an old, old woman in a grey shawl: a crone in a fairy tale. She held up a flower while she—Mary Virginia—stood with her mouth agape (she chose that word carefully now in her new profession), thinking what age could do. That woman would have been young and pretty once, maybe even beautiful: with hopes and dreams. There were always those, weren't there? There she stood pristine, new and virginal in her going-away suit, and Mary Virginia did not care now who knew that, even if it dated her. Back then she thought in pride, at least she'd never be an old, old woman selling something.

That night with Aaron over her, she reached out to touch the rose in its glass. "Ouch," she said when a thorn stuck her. And again later, "Ouch." The next morning a drop of blood on the sheet was the shape of a petal. "Good grief," Aaron had said, raising up. He went on saying that for years till he quit. "Can I help it?" she had said. Her bones knit together, hardly a feather could pass. "It's not personal," she told him. Aaron kept pushing, shoving, groveling inside for years till he quit that too.

Now an old woman, she found in amazement her nipples had risen. Lord, help us, she thought. How many years since—? and she knew longer than since she and Aaron knew one another in a Biblical way. She always had been big-bosomed, a pouter pigeon: not to her liking or taste. Coo-oo, Mary Virginia said to herself as if in a cote. To the menfolks and boys, however, it was a different story. Not that she let anybody touch her before Aaron and that ring was on her finger. Girls didn't give it away in her day, like they did now. If her day had come? Mary Virginia considered all the possibilities for the elderly and ways to keep them going—and going, like that Energizer rabbit on TV, banging a drum and advertising a battery. In that other time, menfolks and boys wanted to "cop a feel." Mary Virginia congratulated herself on knowing that expression, an "in" saying, and she was proud of knowing to say that.

There was a lighthearted feel to being cut in on at dances and held against a male's chest. Aaron said she was pretty, but Mary Virginia knew the reason for her popularity, why the menfolks and boys brushed against her as if by accident. There was not much in the world that did fool her, she thought. One finger tweaked a breast and she cried, Bad! to herself. Memory flashed by. Never a Catholic, she was taught anyway never to touch herself, though found out early on about giving yourself pleasure in the night. She yanked her hand from the blouse's plush material, thinking Bad bad bad as taught. Suppose Aaron turned and caught her in the act? "Playing with myself." She had to whisper the words even to herself, then feeling younger than springtime, hummed the song.

She stepped out finally crying, "Hell-o." And if she told Aaron, I'm coming out of the closet, he would not have the faintest idea she was making a joke. Mary Virginia stuck hands from her sides like a windmill, turning this way/that for his inspection and knew what would happen. Aaron would look up—there he went, his mind reflecting as blankly as a cue ball. His blue-eyed gaze would slowly melt white like hot grease, revealing a lack of comprehension. The moment at hand would pass. She would be left again in an irritation she could hardly stand. Having heard garlic was good for the brain, she made another mental note to buy capsules, then stepped out with perspiration pouring from her hairline.

Aaron looked up. "Get weight off, you wouldn't be hot." He glanced at a window she had cracked open. "I'm shivery."

"Put on some clothes." She did not tell him she was sick of looking at his long, droopy underdrawers and skinny, white legs sticking out. "Uff," she went, blowing hair off her face. She grabbed her knees in pain from having stood so long. "Get fat off, you wouldn't have arthritis either," he said. She hated the way Aaron said "fat" which made her think about blubber, whales and want to blow little bubbles through a snout. His eyes narrowed into a fox's or a fortuneteller's peering into a crystal ball. "I don't know what you are going to do," he said.

"Get my knees replaced like I've been told. I'd have done it by now if I had somebody to stay with you."

"I can stay by myself."

"You can't."

"Can."

"Can't."

"Can so."

Mary Virginia went back to the closet, knowing they'd stay there all day like children going can/can't unless she stopped them, confronting again the safe, dark interior where she and Aaron went when there were tornado warnings. Left alone, he would light the stove and forget or lay on the floor in a dead, low-blood-sugar-level faint. Nobody came visiting any longer, any more than doctors paid house calls. Their son Peter in Memphis might phone or his wife Judy; but before they could get help from sixty miles, things could be in a sorry state only she could straighten out. Judy worked like all sensible women today and no sense sending Aaron up there. He'd be a caged animal anyway in a city for a week and afraid to stick his nose outdoors because of crime. "I'll go to the fair if you drive right," she said.

Aaron was going to say something funny; she geared up for it, put on a fixed grin and stare. He pounded his little men's feet to the floor, toes up and heels going rat-a-tat. She thought men ought to have big feet and wear out-sized brogans. Aaron's shoes in the closet beside her own were no bigger than an elf's. She chose that word carefully too while knowing she might be the only person in the community who knew "fairy" had another meaning. Aaron sang out, "I'll drive to the right coming and going," as if calling a square dance. That was not what she meant and he knew it. She meant for him to drive correctly. Damn, she would have said if she cursed. Now she had to sit beside him again, going, "Don't go around curves on the wrong side, don't cross the middle, don't drive in fits, starts and jerks." Jerk, she thought.

Aaron was called "Mister A." around the countryside by blacks and whites. Out of respect and affection, she guessed. He was a good, square man to blacks long before the idea was popular and the government said you had to be. Once he had been road supervisor and put gravel up to a bunch of folks' front doors. Late in life, he stood at the Baptists' invitational, professing Jesus Christ to be his Savior, saying the first time around his Mamma made him do it and he was too young to understand. There was not a dry eye in the house that night. Words spread over the countryside, Mister A. would be in Paradise when the time came. Para-dee-so, Mary Virginia said to herself, the way she heard it on television.

Aaron was a true Christian. To her knowledge, he had never done an unkind thing on purpose. He would not even put a tick down the toilet to drown as hard as she tried to keep house. Nevertheless anybody seeing his pickup on the road shouted, "Mister A.!" so those walking could jump ditch banks to safety. Maybe people at eighty shouldn't have a driver's license? *What about me in five years?* Mary Virginia panicked at the idea of not having wheels. And "wheels" she repeated to herself in delight at knowing that expression. Did Aaron remember as she did when they, as country kids, drove at the right age to the county courthouse, gave the Chancery clerk a quarter for a license and drove home again? Sometimes his memory seemed faulty.

To take away his license would strip Aaron of the last of manhood, she believed. He was old-fashioned enough to think a man had to do all the driving when a woman was present. He'd still be opening doors for her if she let him. Her one respite in the day was when Aaron drove to the Whitehill cafe for coffee with other retirees. Otherwise, he was in the way. If she vacuumed, she had to say, "Lift your feet." Then he moved as if he had not heard, in a slow, mechanical way like a push-button toy. He bent one knee to his chest with a foot and then the other one, stomping each back down in the same way, unable to hold up two feet at once.

How could you emasculate what had not been up since Hector was a pup? Whoever Hector had been? She always had had to wonder. She did not miss any of that hoo-hah either. Mary Virginia put on shoes, thinking that going to the fair she would be on the right-hand side as passenger and coming home, it would be the same way. What then was the right side of the road? Or even the right road? The road not taken? She smiled at drudging that up from ancient history when she was a girl studying poetry.

She pulled off the light, and Aaron's scalp leapt out as soft and clean, as sweet as a baby's, under hair that was cut too short. Barbers probably gave him peppermints the way they used to give Peter. Maybe she ought to go to the shop with Aaron also? The string in her hand felt slimy but turned loose jumped into the air, alive and well there, dancing. Something dead had come back to life. Another memory surfaced she thought long gone and knew now it never had been. Hands holding her child's thighs went creepy-crawly up in a way she knew even then was wrong. "Don't, Daddy," she had said, wobbling above the crowd. The fingers went on up, touching the biting, elastic edges of her lace panties. She had to wear her best ones going out, her Mother always cautioning, "You might be in a wreck and lay dead showing dirty, old underbritches." A thick finger separated with a scratchy hangnail, probing toward the warm, soft, moist, pink hole belonging only to herself, offering comfort in the night. "Your girlself," he whispered up.

There was a sluicing sound and a low, guttural, deep growl that was not his own. "You like it," he said. "She-devil. Minx."

"I do not. I hate it," she cried. "I hate you."

Down she went tumbling past his eyebrows, nose, mouth, to lie spread-eagled on the ground, her legs as spent and twisted as a rag doll's. Her crotch exposed, she peed as she went. She lay in damp, dirty underpants while people ran crying, "She fell. Little Mary Virginia." Ladies knelt, smelling of damp, honeysuckle talcum powder and men of bay rum and cigarettes. One man held her gently, saying, "Careful. There may be bones broke."

He flailed them away, crying, "Get on. Get off. She's all right."

"You don't know that," the man said. "She fell from a long way up. A woman's softer voice went along behind like undertow. "Why, Henry," she said.

"Ouch," she said when he yanked her by the elbow.

Going home afterwards in the truck, he told her, "Don't pull a stunt like that again." No sense telling him he bent so low over, she had to fall off. He knew that. "Mention anything," he told her, "and you'll be looking up from the bottom of the cistern."

He went behind the barn at home and came back smelling of homebrew, wiping his mouth across one sleeve, his eyes jeering. Her Mother's turned the same white, fearful, lonesome color, knowing Mary Virginia caused something but she'd bear the brunt of another bender.

Until this many years later, her own eyes reflected in the mirror the same lackluster color of cucumbers. Little boys poked at her elbow cast, crying, "Wet your britches and we saw. Five years old and wet your pants." Little girls remained aloof and snooty, told not to play with a child who'd scream she hated her Daddy and in public.

Aaron on the bed now sat as listlessly as that first evening in Pensacola. In her reddened mind's eye, Mary Virginia saw again planes breaking sound barriers and heard ships belching in the night. Aaron had turned from the shy, modest man she married into an ogre, wanting on top, red-faced and sweaty, trying to stick a finger where only hers ought to go. No more invasions, she told herself. *Maybe never.* That was the night he first crawled off, saying, "Good grief."

She tied on shoes now as fresh, white and new as her blouse, smiling beatifically above both. Aaron said, "What's on your feets? Your feets too big."

She stood still. Something was missing, something left out of that old song, and she could not think what. "Sneakers," she said. "What do you think?"

He cut across her with a smirk, saying, "Clodhoppers? Boats?" And while she told him, "Everybody wears sneakers," he said, "Your Grand-momma wore Army boots," dredging that up from the old World War II joke book when it was not funny even back then. "For comfort," she said, unlike the old days her Mother talked about when you did not go anywhere without hats, gloves and your best girdle on.

Mary Virginia rubbed one shoe atop the other to muss them up, saying, "They look so—," and paused again professionally to choose the right word, opting for "important," avoiding what Aaron would have chosen, "big," and ended, "because they're new."

Aaron unfolded himself and got up. She waited in front of TV while he dressed, her purse upright on her knees as stiffly as terrier's ears, waiting for three knocks of his razor to mean he finished. A *Mary Tyler Moore* re-run was on, the woman's buck teeth as tiresome as ever. How did some people make it so big without much talent or looks? In show *biz*, Mary Virginia remembered. Break a leg, Mary, she told her in secret.

One two three: she counted and her shoulders went slack. Aaron rambled in back of the house, opening and closing closet doors and drawers. When he came back, it was her turn to rise up, saying, "Good grief." Aaron wore the same and she let herself go ahead and think it—*shit*-eating grin he wore earlier, a cat chomping canary feathers, as if something great, big and important was going to happen when the fair was not all that much: toss some ping-pong balls into water and—. Oh no, she thought: not again. She told him as much, "Listen here, boy. Don't come home wagging me another goldfish to take care of. Toss your balls at something else."

When Aaron started laughing, she said, "Hush your mouth. You ought to be ashamed." Then she stared at his feet and said, "Oh no. You're not."

"Why not? Me in my shoes. You in yours."

Mary Virginia shoved her feet forward, knowing she could not change Aaron's mind-set: stubborn as a mule, dumb as a bat. Women older than she wore sneakers, but he was going to make a fool of himself. He had dragged out from somewhere, and she wondered where on earth, a pair of brown and white shoes so old they were grayed and cracked. She remembered the difficulty of finding saddle oxfords in wartime and their importance in the midst of so much else. If Aaron had them, what else did he have she did not know about? Nothing, stupid, she told herself: somebody he'd been married to fifty-five years who looked into his stool every morning. She knew about the stabbed, crumbling butterfly collection in the attic; the boy's scarred baseball and mitt; the skinny old, moth-eaten navy uniform.

Aaron was going not down the drain, she remembered, but down the tube. Did that mean as in television? He was topped also with a golfer's cap like players seen on TV. Where had he gotten that cap and why, when he had never held a club in his life? Then she remembered his buying it at a yard sale while she looked at dishes. She had turned—and there he stood. Grinning like a banshee, he was as la-de-dah as if they were country club members. He was handsome; she had to admit that. Other women stared. But then was then and now is now, she thought. They rode home afterwards with the dishes rattling while she told him, "Aaron, you can't wear that hat."

"Why not?"

Had it really been necessary to say because you don't play golf? She only glared out the window. They strayed on through the silent, green countryside, reaching the main road through town before Aaron took off that cap, folding it quietly into a pocket. He returned to wearing his John Deere cap, as befit a farmer. He wore now, too, a joke birthday tie from Peter, long stashed away. The tie was big, blue and white polka-dotted, and stuck from either side of his chin like oversized cat's whiskers. Aaron must have gone crazy, sauntering across the floor in something like a waltz, tippy-toeing this way and that. She got up, saying, "Turn off the set." He was always leaving it on, another reason not to leave him alone if she had her knees fixed. And of course she was going to do that! Hippety-hop, Mary Virginia thought. She'd be out dancing before anybody knew what happened. Let him stay home alone, burning the house down and himself with it.

He came back with the chastened, humbled air old men get as if all they wanted in life was to be told what to do by women, that and nothing else, and were glad to be rid of macho ways they'd had to adopt, to cope, and were sorry about now, embarrassed, too, they could no longer perform as men probably even for themselves, squinched-up as they tried, nor drive a nail straight or a tractor row, like a good, big, friendly shaggy dog ready to do your bidding. She thought about giving Aaron a pat. Their test-tas, whatever it was called, played out, the way women gave out of estrogen. Only that could be replaced, she thought, smugly.

Mary Virginia got out of the way when Aaron came back in what he must think was a two-step, one foot slipping ahead of the other one, when Aaron had never danced through a whole note in his life and not because he was Baptist either. He just could not keep time to Ride-A-Cock-Horse. Nighttime images rose of sitting by Pensacola dance floors while others "cut a rug." If back then she thought herself longing for a dance partner, maybe what she'd really been longing for was another partner through life. . . .

No longer did she see herself in chunky Eleanor Powell shoes but gliding, and ever swiftly gliding, over waxed dance floors held in arms with braid, like rich, elderly widows on TV cruises. The women always found themselves another fellow, and maybe the captain, because the shows were hogwash TV and not reality. Reality was tables full of winsome, gray-haired ladies eating at Shoney's when she and Aaron went there in Nashtoba for their own supper on Friday evenings. The Memphis paper recently ran an article about the trend toward older women and younger men. She pooh-poohed that idea, saying the trend would last about as long as a feather in a fire. When the rich widow's husband's money was gone, so would the young man be. Coattails flew away in her mind's eye. Mary Virginia turned with the sudden thought there were women in this world with their own resources. There had been the Doris Duke person and the sad, faded heiress whose son got killed, who married a movie star and a prince and ended up paying alimony. Was that fair? She turned to ask Aaron, and had the sudden idea he might look back, saying, Why not? And why not? she thought. Was she not as much on the side of women's lib as she thought?

Mary Virginia knew she avoided the new doctor in Whitehill, not because Dr. Key was Korean, another alien in a country that didn't need any, but because she was female. Simply, she came up in a time not knowing women doctors and could not adjust to the idea one knew enough to treat her. In the same way, she would not go to a man in a beauty parlor. She would not have gone to a female lawyer for love nor money and resented the young women coming out of law school with swingy hair and degrees. She told Peter it was ridiculous Judy was studying to be a paralegal. She had a good enough job in Goldsmith's home-decorating studio.

Aaron went by crooning, whiskers shaking, "Have you ever seen a dream walking," and she came back of the bounding words, finishing,

"Well, I have." Behind the blackened TV with its stilled voices was only a memory, like dead people. She got into the car beside Aaron, having watched him watch her coming down the steps, sideways, grasping the iron railing, one foot, one heavy hip lumbering after the other one and more like a bear, she reckoned, than any animal she had thought of yet.

When he looked away, she said, "You didn't have a bowel movement this morning," and she thought, *ergo* from another puzzle. "Therefore," she said, "if you don't go by tonight, I've got to give you something. Better stop at the store." He nosed down the driveway and headed uptown on the wrong side of the road. "Look out," she screamed as a pickup clipped past. Town had a silvery trailer beside the road now that was a bank. Inside the front window a teller frequently phoned, saying, "Mister A's nearly done it again. Almost caused a head-on." Or Aaron had nearly mowed down a pedestrian, a dog or somebody on a horse. Sometimes the teller reported, "He's had him another sinking spell. He's sitting on the store steps." It was fortunate then only one store was left to town. She could phone, saying, "Shall I come get him? Or can he get up?"

As Aaron pulled to the store, Mary Virginia thought about Judy, knowing if something happened to her, the girl would slap her in a home in a heartbeat. Her vagina muscles tightened. Whose wouldn't, thinking about living in the Sunset Rest Home? She determined that minute to fool and outwit them, to live on and on, live to be a hundred, longer, live forever. They'd bill her as the dancing grandma, the literary great-grand. There would be an appearance on the *Good Morning America* show, talking through a little black mike clipped to her dress. Yes, I was a homemaker, she would say. Lo, these many years. Then I had a career change late in life. Very late, she would add, sparkling, little old lady's blue eyes twinkling. Willard Scott, or his equivalent, would say, as he always said about such women, She's still pur-ty as a picture. Maybe by then she'd have courage to say, Bullshit. We look like a bunch of wrinkled cantaloupes.

The President would send greetings. And maybe by the twenty-first century, too, they'd have stopped electing sexpots. A woman's magazine might give her a makeover. She always had wondered how you got so lucky. They would restyle her hair, feather in her brows better, add glitter. Accompanying articles always said, We brought out her eyes. Knowing nothing of cosmetics, she feared stopping by a counter and having a snippy salesgirl blanch at her appearance and make her wrinkles worse by filling them in with foundation. Mary Virginia tightened her seat belt; Aaron's lay lax on the seat between them. "Some people think you're better off without these," she said.

"You can't get thrown clear in an accident," he said.

"A fat lot of good that did those folks strewn over highway 51 the other morning," she said. Aaron would know the accident she meant because that was all the community had talked about for days. "Ten people in one car and all killed," she said. That many folks in one car meant rednecks or blacks, but nobody wanted such an accident to happen. "Carnage," *The Democrat* called it, and she shuddered, thinking the word. She said, "Nobody knows what happened. Or even who was driving."

When Aaron said nothing, she wondered again if his hearing was not going. A cluster of balloons tacked ahead to a telephone pole showed the way to the fair, yellow and pink ones, little suns and little moons. She was glad she and Aaron knew their countryside and did not have to gawk out windows, like idiots, asking directions. People stopped on the roads and asked questions seemed like signalmen on the old navy warships, raising and lowering their arms, answering them. She got out at the store, thinking, I am sore afraid. There were hoodlums moving into the community now, tacky, motorcycle people fleeing crime in Memphis. She learned about their gangs from TV. Aaron said you couldn't trust a single fellow who rode one, and when she said, grinning, she'd like to have trusted Marlon Brando, Aaron said Brando wouldn't have wasted his water on her. Then shocked as he'd intended, Mary Virginia said, "Just be ugly."

Who was ugly now was the fellow zooming by so fast he rustled her pants' legs, in a deep, black helmet like a death's head and only needing a sickle. All the drivers wore the same silvery-blue goggles, like mirrors, reflecting the countryside, high, wide, handsome sky and trees made curly by kudzu, revealing everything but the drivers' eyes and who they were, devil or friend, male or female. They gave her the same uneasy sense as limousines on the highway with blacked-out windows, so that you did not know who was inside, if anybody. Hooded falcons on nature programs gave her the same sense of foreboding; they did not seem to be thinking birdlike thoughts up under there but something evil and sinister. The fellow streaking past now was a hideous hunchback, his shirt billowing out. A girl clung on behind, her ponytail flying. What else is new? Mary Virginia asked herself. All the girls had one. She culled that expression off the *Bill Cosby Show*. So what else is new? she was always asking Aaron, who never answered.

The girl cupped to the boy like a teaspoon as if all she had in life was clinging onto some man. *Poor thing.* Aaron stood, staring after the girl's flying hair or either after her round "bee-hind" disappearing in tight, black britches. Mary Virginia had the curious thought he had a hand down a pants' pocket, playing with something down there floppy as a hound. Don't be silly, girl, she told herself. *On the main road through town?*

Maybe it's s-o-a-r afraid? she thought, knowing she ought to know her Bible better. She asked Aaron, "Is it s-o-a-r or s-o-r-e afraid?" and when he did not answer, she determined again to see about his hearing. They went up into a store with the shelves nearly bare. The new owner reputedly lost all his money at the riverboat gambling casinos recently put in on the Mississippi in Tunica County, just the way diehard religious folks predicted would happen when the casinos went in. Aaron, ahead of her, dodged counters and bins, barely missing some of them. She went up close behind, smelling Old Spice aftershave and said, "Aaron, what do you see when you're driving?" then wished she had not asked because he told her. "A great white orbit like the sun coming down in the middle of the road," Aaron said, bringing to mind a manifestation of Jesus.

"Kudzu," he said. "Hanging all around, it makes you go into and out of shadows."

Mary Virginia stared into his cloudy vision. "I wish you'd had your cataract operations when they were using lasers. It's supposed to be better." She read off labels. "Milk of Magnesia. Cod Liver Oil. They ought to have something newer." A couple came in wearing sporty fishing clothes, probably Memphis people camping over on the government dam. Such people always wore the same sheepish grins about having discovered this quaint country store. "Out of another century. Fabulous," a woman once whispered. Mary Virginia still smarted over her remarks.

This one today said, "Have you any olive oil?" and Mary Virginia said to herself in her best kitchey-koo little girl's voice, "Ooo my, yes."

"Yes 'um," the owner said. "It's over yonder on the medicine shelf."

"Medicine? I wanted salad oil."

"Yes 'um, I know. But folks in these parts don't spend that kind of money on salad dressing. They heat up olive oil for earaches."

"Oh, I see it," the woman said slowly, taking a bottle. The husband poked her ribs to keep her from laughing. Aaron went about in his usual oblivious way, buying Gummy Bears. The woman turned from paying and faced Mary Virginia, who pulled her ears sideways from her head like Mickey Mouse and lolled out her tongue, playing loco country bumpkin. "My word," the woman said after another look at Aaron's clothes and went out, looking back scared.

Mary Virginia, carrying Ex-Lax to the counter, was pleased by her own inventiveness, which a writer must have. "This day ain't nobody's play pretty," the owner said. "You sweatin' like a nigger writin' a love letter."

She stood horrified by such a joke in this day and age. Why was it not as funny, saying, A white man?—But it was not, and she knew that. Because, she thought, blacks had always been sexier and freer people until whites started acting like them, living together openly and having babies without benefit of matrimony. If it was one, a benefit? She knew sorrowful tales from that other time about girls in this community, having to give up babies. They reminded her still of haunted, blackened souls wandering the earth, looking for children they gave away. Yet still out of that same old blocked past, she had to say, "It's at election."

Aaron passed by, gumming, and said, "It's at meetin'."

"It's not," she cried, so loudly the owner gave Aaron an embarrassed stare, and he could not look back from under his cap brim.

"Tis," he muttered.

"Tis not," she cried, then grabbed up her package, thinking in this day and age she and Aaron never would have married. They might have gone together because of the proximity of living in a small town. But the war had brought on urgency. *Urgency*, she thought another time, like mourning. People did things back then they might otherwise not have done. War had commanded your life and the thinking was anybody going to it would be killed. She had been in love actually with someone her parents did not want her to marry. Brad Richards was from the Delta, with the stigma attached any boy from there had: that he was wild as a buck. Her parents did not know his parents, and that kind of thing carried weight back then. Brad came to Itna Homa, visiting, and then returned regularly to court, driving an old Studebaker and literally through hell and high water. The levees back then were not high enough to keep water off the Delta's flat land. She came closer to sin on the back seat of that old car than before or since, and suspected her parents knew that. She broke off with Brad Richards the way they wanted.

She and Aaron continued their same placid dating of ten years, both dragging feet of clay. Then Aaron was going overseas and she could not let him go alone. She would have to go as far as Florida with him. They stood up before a Justice of the Peace one weekend, with only their parents. She had not known for years Aaron was AWOL: so homesick he simply hitched off from his naval station in Millington, Tennessee. Now, it seemed to her his finest, bravest, shining hour. Nothing so spectacular had happened since then. Aaron never got over his terrible homesickness—even having both their mammas come visit Florida did not help—just as she never got over feeling something missing from having no real wedding. She supposed, even now, she wanted to toss a bouquet to a gaggle of bridesmaids.

Brad wrote a few letters which she never answered. That withholding gave her a sense of one-upmanship, the way withholding sex from boys did back then. He probably still wondered what happened to the buxom, pretty country girl he courted but couldn't capture. Those tissue-thin, V-mail letters arriving with his APO address gave her the first startled sense of being a nearly ignorant, simple country girl living in a no-place, nothing address in Mississippi, while he at her age was seeing the world. She determined some day to go see all those places herself.

She never asked her parents what they thought about how things turned out. Brad came back from service to open a dairy store in Memphis, which became a chain. His name was now all over the city; he was big man up there, top dog. And married to him, she would be a Memphis society matron.

In the rear of the store men sat at a snack bar, a recent innovation. When they put it in, Aaron said, "Folks used to cook at home." And she told him, "Boy, I still do. What's wrong with you." The men called out, teasing him about his costume. "Hey, dude." Then one man continued over his barbecue sandwich, "It might-a-been the steering gear let loose." Mary Virginia went closer. "Any news?"

"You can still see the skid marks where it happened," the man said. "Folks from the folks' church put up ten little white crosses."

"Traffic's gotten to be something else around here with folks racing to Tunica," a man said. "I've come out of that side road by the new Wal-Mart's and nearly run the stop sign. Overrun with kudzu. The county don't keep up its road work."

"Seems like the car was trying to avoid something," a man said. "The bridge guardrail is tore plumb to pieces."

"Folks who would put that many folks in a car are liable to have had a kid driving. Or something," Aaron said.

All the country people agreed. One man said, "I wish we could sic that vine back on Japan. It stopped erosion but swallowed us up. A plot to get back because of the war, I believe." Everybody laughed.

They were going, and Joe Veazey said, "Good to have seen you, Aaron." Mary Virginia wondered where Joe had been if not there for coffee every morning. She could not remember his wife Josie as having been anywhere. On the porch, she said, "I'm glad you didn't see that accident, Aaron. If it had been any closer to Whitehill, that time of morning you would have."

Aaron was still gumming Gummy Bears and said nothing. They drove on the distance of half a city block in Memphis, which was town, and turned where the balloons indicated. When the road wound into a curve, Aaron stopped. "You get out," he said, "and I'll park."

Mary Virginia climbed out, pressing hands to her thighs, and started up an incline. A passing townsman offered an elbow, saying, "Hep you?" and when she told him, "No," he shrugged and said, "Suit yourself," which made her even madder.

Beyond the lodge at the top of the hill, there was nothing but the slow, aged hills and pasture land with cows huddled together. They made her think briefly of the need of everything for something else, and of how Peter resented being an only child. Age made her have only him. In wartime, she and Aaron were thought old to get married and today would be kids. She stared down from the hill's crumbly, yellow edge, thinking what she saw was mostly what she knew of the world. She would not have married Aaron if she knew he would live nowhere else. When they left for Florida, she thought, This is all. This is it. We'll never be back for good.

She would have stayed forever with palm trees and an ocean, and used to stare endlessly off at the horizon, blue and blinding, dreaming of going to Europe. Aaron with tears in his eyes talked of nothing but home, and home was here where she stood in these blue, shaded hills. Their first Christmas, they went swimming. All day long, Aaron jumped in waves, singing, "M-I-crooked-letter-crooked-letter-I-crooked-letter-I-humpback-humpback-I spells Miss'sippi!"

A woman from Maine joined in, singing, "I'm Dreaming of a White Christmas." She and Aaron embraced, jumping, choking, swallowing, singing on raggedly like drunken people.

I should have told him, Watch out on the road. Mary Virginia looked back down, thinking Aaron would not be careful enough. He came along in a spate of people, like a bedraggled small army. She had not thought before, Suppose something happened to Aaron? He was talking excitedly to a peroxide blonde and not as if they had just met. But was it possible Aaron knew somebody she did not, even from out in the county? The woman was younger, but not all that much younger. Settle-aged, Mary Virginia decided. And nobody had hair that color naturally at her age, or any other time. It was shingled up the sides and sat out flat on top in a new style Mary Virginia hated, but which she knew was "far out."

The woman stumbled, and Aaron caught her. Her shoes were ridiculous for the country road, even if feminine and pretty, wedgies with heels striped lavender and green. Her pants suit was light pink and Mary Virginia thought again about the whole ensemble, Far out. She stumbled herself and in the moment of righting herself felt abandoned, adrift in air, a bird falling, a plane plummeting, and stood finally with her heart pounding, looking around for safety's sake. "Mary Virginia, you need a cane. We watched you come up that hill." Ruby Morgan patted a seat beside her, and Mary Virginia headed the direction of her canasta group, a bunch of country-looking women under trees, like me, she guessed, though she never wore polyester. "I'm not there yet," she said about the cane, and the women exchanged looks. She had never noticed before how close up beside her nose Ruby's little eyes were, like a ferret's. "Who's that?" she asked about the woman.

In a moment someone answered,—"Letty Pegrum's sister." And when Mary Virginia started saying, "Who—?" the woman cut in sharply. "Mary Virginia, you try to be so savvy. You know Letty owns The Golden Goose over to Nashtoba.

"Oh. I forgot."

"Because none of us goes there," Lucy Craig said. "Who'd pay those prices to have snotty town women look down on you for living out in the county. I've heard women go in there to get their toenails painted. Wouldn't you think they could think up some other way to waste money?"

"The sister married early-on and went up north," a woman said. "Her husband just passed and she came back down to be Letty's manicurist. They live out on the road beside the new Wal-Mart's."

Mary Virginia wanted to tell her nobody said "passed" but black people. But she said, "Why does a woman cut her hair like a man's?"

"With her figure she doesn't have to worry," Allie McCall said. "Beauty parlor people always have the latest. That haircut's in."

Mary Virginia stared at Allie, the crossword puzzle friend, knowing she'd have learned the use from one of them. They worked a puzzle from the Memphis paper over the telephone every morning. "I know the *scenario*," she said, thinking Allie would not know that one. She picked up the use, flipping past a sexy program on cable TV once. "The haircut may be in. But who'd want it?"

"Those that have got it, I reckon," Ruby said. "Nobody hog-tied 'em."

"What's her name?"

"Hon, don't—," Ruby started.

"Let's go eat," Allie McCall said. "I can't smell that catfish frying any longer without having some."

"I believe I have heard the name called," a woman said and finally dredged up, "Michele. What's Aaron dolled up as?"

"He thinks he looks so cute," Mary Virginia said. She needed to get up, too, with her knees aching and head him away from the goldfish booth. Only Aaron was not headed that direction, or hers either when she sat waiting to tell him, Bring me a coke. She would start with a diet one and maybe weight would begin to slip off. She was furious the women had watched her walk up that hill and talked about it.

Aaron at least passed the sign reading Five Balls for 25¢, though he could come back. He and she, the woman, went around a tent where Mary Virginia could no longer see them. Every year Aaron had to win himself that goldfish. She heard in her head now *Plop* as if a ping-pong ball hit water. Then he came home with it like a trophy as if tossing a ping-pong ball into a goldfish bowl he had really, really done something. He was never interested in the fish afterwards, and she either fed them all too much or not enough. But she had enough little goldfish bowls and did not want to encounter another dead fish floating on water, looking at her with one dead black eye, accusingly. The last fish slipped down a drain while she changed its water. Wait! she screamed, but the glittery tail eluded her. She determined the fish swam away through a complicated, interlocking drainage system to free itself at last in the Gulf of Mexico. *Olé*, Mary Virginia said to herself, in her mind's eye wearing a ruffled skirt and snapping castanets. The fish swam on freely, she thought, huge and golden in an ocean, never to be a little fish again.

Olé was the answer recently to a puzzle question about a matador. She and Allie then discussed Ava Gardner's famous fling with one, wondering if Ava would have been better off staying a simple farm girl in North Carolina rather than ending up a famous ex-movie star dying lonesomely in a foreign city. Allie voted, Yea. Mary Virginia, Nay. The woman had a life at least, she said, even if she had to marry a bantam rooster like Mickey Rooney to get it.

"Aaron looks adorable." A croaky cigarette voice spoke behind them. Ruby turned a stiff neck, saying, "Hello, Letty." All the canasta women had old-age complaints when they'd started out together as young marrieds. "We were just talking about beauty parlors and the new haircut that's so chick."

"Sheeek," Mary Virginia breathed out, without Ruby's knowing she was being corrected. Letty smiled, waving tolerant red fingernails, and went off. Mary Virginia wondered how they looked to her, a bunch of country women under trees, knees spread, laps fallen, her own thighs spread over a chair. They all had the same cropped curls, pepper and salt once, now mostly white. They all went to Mabel Wilkin's each week, who had one sink and a dryer in her house. And no framed gilt certificate on the wall either, advertising graduation from a beauty school, Mary Virginia thought. Mabel still stuck you under a dryer with a large hair net that left red welts across your forehead. Blowing dry had not hit Itna Homa. These days they were doing their own hair; Mabel was laid up with what a doctor gave a fancy name to, carpel tunnel syndrome, while the rest of them called it a swollen wrist. "Josie, where have you and Joe been?"

"You know we don't go nowhere, Mary Virginia. How come you to ask a thing like that?"

Mary Virginia could not remember and stared into her lap, then recalled the store but said anyway, "I don't know." She shrugged. "How'd that woman get to be called Michele in this part of the country? She must have changed it."

"Hon," Ruby said, "forget it."

"Come on," Allie said, clapping her hands. "Aren't we going to eat? Can you make it, Mary Virginia?"

Angry at being singled out, Mary Virginia said, "Of course," and struggled up, thinking fried fish, fried hush puppies, fried potatoes, and she'd eat them all up the way she did every year.

"Look-a-yonder who that is."

A woman spoke, and everyone turned. Here came Brad Richards up the incline, as large as life, looking exactly as he did on TV ads:

like a combination between Kentucky Fried's Colonel Sanders and a Confederate General: flowing hair, white suit and black string tie. We used to go together, Mary Virginia thought of muttering, but nobody would hear or pay attention. She and Aaron had been too long in their data banks as a couple, she supposed.

"What's he doing here?" Ruby whispered. A hush had fallen over the crowd. A thrall—a pall? Mary Virginia could not remember what she was trying to think about. Brad came on up among others, laughing, talking, and waving a benevolent hand like the Pope blessing commoners. "They might be using his ice cream," Ruby said, still whispering. Mary Virginia thought the words *sotto voce* from another puzzle, and let little blanks fill in her mind.

"He's got kin out in the county he still comes to visit," a woman said. The canasta women swarmed toward him in a horde, and Brad gave them the abashed grin of celebrities trying to pretend they're not being noticed, while glad to be. Several of the women surged past him, more interested in feeding their stomachs, and several remained behind to stand with Mary Virginia. "Hey there," she said, stepping up close.

He gazed down fearfully, his eyes asking, What does this old woman, this biddy, want? He stared after the women who had left, obviously wishing this one had gone too. "Ma'm." He made a quick, polite brush into air after a hat that was not present. "Still a tease," she told him, rising onto her toes as much as possible, wrinkling her nose. "Cute as a button," he once said. He had to stand ground, being gracious to older women in this part of the country. He swallowed his Adam's apple, his eyes still querying, What do you want?

She turned her hands out to show him nothing, nothing at all,—see, no scrap of paper, no autograph book, only her purse strap hung over one wrist, limply like a snake. He said, "Hey," looking brighter. "You girls heard about my bargain days up in Memphis?" and he spelled that out, "D-a-z-e. Best prices on dairy products you'll ever have."

"We can't make it up to Memphis any longer."

"Hush up, Ruby," Mary Virginia said. "Some of us can." Brad ran a hand with a large signet ring over carefully colored, yellow-white hair. "You'll have to excuse me," he said. "I meet so many—. Getting old. Forgetful."

"So what else is new?" Ruby asked, with a sideways glance at Mary Virginia. They began to lead her away, tugging gently, lovingly even, whispering, "Mary Virginia." She huffed herself against them like a bird huddling under its own wings, against rain. Would she have known Brad if she had not seen him on TV? He was older and grayer but strangely unchanged, the way men can age, his face like paraffin. Maybe he'd had it lifted? "Anile" sprang to her mind, a word she hated seeing even in print: old womanish, hag, it meant. And she refused to think "crone." She looked harder behind his ears to see if there were scars.

He suddenly stuck out a hand with business cards splayed between the fingers. "Take one," he said. "They're signed. Give one to a clerk in any of my stores and get a free gallon of ice cream." Mary Virginia brushed against hers and let it fall to the ground. She could have kicked Ruby's butt when she picked it up. Little girls who had hung back came up, their faces painted to look like hoydens or child prostitutes. Their mothers ought to make them stay fresh, wholesome looking and innocent as long as possible, Mary Virginia thought, longing back. A child tugged at his coat, and Brad leaned down without a sigh, creak or groan. He straightened without a whimper, tugging his beard, saying, "Like Santa. Why, thank you."

The child snuggled against him as sure of her acceptance as a kitten or puppy. What nerve! Mary Virginia thought. How did that child know what she herself might not yet know? She had never known how to cotton up to somebody but used vinegar, acid, to get what she wanted. Because her parents had kept her squashed down, beaten to the quick, and she had to fight back up. Put up your dukes, she thought from some old comic strip. If not for boobs and a pretty face, she might have gotten—why—nobody. Suddenly there was a surge of gratitude toward Aaron for taking her as she was. Life with him was not so bad; and if he never set the world on fire, so what? It was too late for that. She had what a million women would give their eyeteeth for.

"Watch out. What on earth."

The fair became a shambles. A sports car slammed into their midst, which was strictly forbidden. A hand-printed sign below said not to drive up. Deep down inside somewhere behind the wheel, people discovered a driver. She stepped out with long, tanned legs in Bermuda shorts, cameras slung around her neck. A placard in her windshield read PRESS, which gave you the right to do anything, Mary Virginia guessed. The crowd having scattered fanned back in. Men hovered, inspecting the car, wondering what good it did you, it was so little. "How come folks buy Japanese," a man asked, "when we had to whup those little devils? Young folks today don't know anything about it."

Pearl Harbor. Blue Pacific isles. Images rose to mind Mary Virginia thought long forgotten, places never visited. Older people present wore facial expressions reflecting history and their part in it. Another man kicked a tire. "I didn't feel like a hero coming back from the war," he said. "But these young fellows back from Vietnam can't stop writing books, making motion pictures, agitating about what was done to them."

Brad remained while others drifted away. Mary Virginia stayed rooted, wanting to bask in his glory. Only now his eyes bulged and his lips were actually wet with saliva. Old goat, she wanted to screech. He ogled; he leered. Familiar puzzle words came back as he watched the girl. Had Aaron ever danced her such attendance, or did it take May/December for that to happen? Where was Aaron when she needed him and not some hick offering an elbow, saying, "Hep you?" "Chick," Ruby had said. "Don't go nowhere." Josie. How came she to feel she did not belong where she was planted? And suddenly Mary Virginia told herself the answer: Because you would never have been satisfied anywhere. You don't fit. You like to nag and complain. The only life's experience that ever gave her satisfaction was having a handicap sticker for her car. She drove with an important air into places other cars had to pass by. Toot, toot, she said under her breath, mentally thumbing her nose at other drivers.

The photographer stood talking in a rapid, high, carrying voice. She was writing a story about country customs fast disappearing, and had yet to find a tent revival. She was covering the fair for the county paper. Hooray! people might have shouted. They were going to be in *The Democrat.* They acted like people anywhere, sashaying about, touching wet fingertips to their eyebrows, pulling in their stomachs. Children present were witches, clowns and skeletons, and those in sheets, Mary Virginia assumed, were ghosts and not the Ku Klux Klan, though no blacks were present to object. In older days, barred, blacks would have enjoyed the rinky-dink games if they'd had a nickel or dime to spare. Now that they could go anywhere, anywhere at all they wanted, they were over at the casinos, squandering their paychecks like everybody else. Where the Klan met now, or convened, she read, was up in Connecticut. It seemed typical of Yankees to criticize the South over what they were guilty of themselves.

The girl cried in her lavish manner she was here to cover the Cutest Couple Contest. The who? The what? The where? "They got to think up some new mess every year to keep folks coming," a man said. "The voting booth's over yonder." He pointed to the tent where Aaron and the woman disappeared. But so long ago? He simply left her like a wet dishrag nobody wanted, a wallflower nobody asked to dance. She remembered going past humiliated classmates seated in their flounced, long dresses, always in somebody's arms, and feeling sorry for them. This is not going to be my end, Mary Virginia thought, ready to stamp her feet. Didn't Aaron remember those old days and her popularity? Didn't Brad Richards? He had not forgotten; he was only mad because she didn't answer his war letters. She went up closer, under his nose, again on her toes as much as possible, and said, "You do so know me, old ten eighty-three seven," proud of an aged memory that recalled his APO number.

He reared back, nostrils flaring, eyes rolling, like a cornered horse on its hind legs, forelegs flailing air. What did she want now, this old biddy, ranting in numbers, or Chinese, her voice high and tinkly in the bridge of her nose like wind chimes? Mary Virginia heard it there. Or speaking in tongues, raving and ranting like the crazy sanctified folks. Faith healers, she thought, when hers in everything was wavering, ebbing, slowly sinking, despite her well-worn presence in Sunday school and church every week. The Baptists had a stained glass window in her honor now for having taught Sunday school forty years. She would like to go give it a smash with a brick as a Halloween trick.

It was her job now to save Brad Richards from himself, someone from her age group and class. Otherwise, he would make a fool out of himself, she thought. That girl would rebuff him and cause him public humiliation and grief. She remained still, as close to his face as she could, and sang, "Rac—ing with the moo—nn. HIGH—," when the others stopped her. "Mary Virginia, he doesn't remember. Can't she face that?"

"She doesn't want to," someone said. But they did not understand this was their very own favorite song, sung just the way their favorite singer did it. "—up in the midnight blue—oo," she finished. "It's the heat," Ruby told him. "It doesn't set right with her arthritis medicine."

"Then I'd take her home and put a cold compress on her head," Brad said.

"Come on, hon," Ruby said. "Let's get that cold coke you've been wanting Aaron to bring you." The women went away, carrying her softly with them. Brad strode across the fairgrounds, long legs striking past one another like garden shears. The girl turned and saw him, beaming a smile of recognition. Imagine meeting a celebrity at this hick place, she meant. A camera rushed to her face and click click click, it went, flash flash flash. Her untethered boobs shook softly in her tee-shirt. Her fluoride smile said if she immortalized him for *The Democrat*, he might get her a job on the Memphis paper or in one of his commercials. There had to be something a girl her age could get out of what a man his age would want: money or a stiff leg up some ladder. Suddenly she remembered something alluded to on TV once that made her turn and ask Aaron, "What is oral sex?" thinking a country boy who had been in the navy might know more than he ought to. When he gave her a hint, she said, "Human beings! I can hardly believe that." Now she recalled an article turned open beside the potty when she went to inspect that about eighty year olds in a Florida retirement community, bringing home AIDS to their wives from prostitutes. She wondered what wives that age were doing still spreading their legs.

"This fair's ruined," Ruby said. "This time next year there'll be a hundred girls just like her, hoping to meet him."

They passed by him going toward the tent, and Mary Virginia stopped to cry, "Just remember this, Brad Richards. The young colt has the fastest step, but the old horse knows the road." Laughter broke out like a shower of Roman candles and she stood in that bright midst, saying, "You do so know me. I was Mary Virginia Alexander."

"Oh, yes," he said, with a little smile on his face. "I believe I do know you." And with his back turned, he went off with other people.

"Mary Virginia, stand up," Ruby said. "You're the one always saying we look like a bunch of wrinkled cantaloupes."

"Step up, ladies. Get in your votes." A townsman sat by a tent flap, handing out pencils and pieces of paper. Mary Virginia stuck the point of hers to her tongue and then the pencil behind one ear, like TV reporters. She voted for a young man in Itna Homa who taught at Nashtoba's Junior College, and had to vote for his wife, who taught also, but wore her skirts entirely too short to be around black male students. Music played on tapes inside the tent, and the women stood in that gloom, saying how nice not to have amplification, their ears assaulted, the way the younger generation liked. Music from their day was so much better; they talked about the old fellows, Harry James, Glenn Miller, Tommy Dorsey. They talked about the pinup of the day, Betty Grable, James' wife, on the noses of bombers and the lockers of all the service boys. She ended up, a woman said who read a book, a drunken blonde hanging around bars with her ex-husband not even responding when she needed help. There was the blonde bombshell of the day, Betty Hutton, found years later as a reformed alcoholic cooking for a bunch of monks. There had been the Peek-a-boo girl, Veronica Lake, with the long slash of hair across one eye, which women wanted to shove back and men liked, found years later as a waitress in New York City. "I'm glad," Ruby said, "I never had any ambitions in this world."

Mary Virginia turned away. There was a wooden platform set up as a dance floor in the dimness, with jiggling, dancing shadows, silhouettes in the dusk. Carrie Jones said, "There's—," and hushed. But there was no way to spare Mary Virginia. Aaron was clearly visible, dancing with Michele. "I thought you always said Aaron couldn't dance," Carrie said. "He looks good to me. Did you try—patience, Mary Virginia?"

Michele guided Aaron through old tunes and jitterbug steps, talking quietly to his face. He swung her outward and under his raised arm. She came back in a slow, wiggling way like a worm straight to his face, her mouth stuck out like a smooch. Aaron, nodding, swung her under his arm again and passed beneath it himself, till they came together. People applauded, standing around their edges. They applauded Aaron's stamina; he was not wearing down. His whiskers jounced, his cap rose and fell, his shoelaces stayed tied. Clearly they were old, familiar partners and had not just met. The others knew that. It was obvious from their stances and averted looks. Mary Virginia stood, knowing the greatest sense of humiliation and rejection only an older woman can feel.

All that while whistling and shuffling at home, Aaron was practicing to meet—who, his Sweetie? Was that what he called her? What in the name of Sam Hill did he call her? Mary Virginia wondered. Practicing at home because all along he had been practicing elsewhere and where but at that woman's house. And for how long, since Wal-Mart's was built? She remembered that was where the woman lived, on the road alongside it. Aaron drove that far alone to do his little shopping at discount, Old Spice, bird seed, fertilizer—and they might have met in the aisles, where Michele would already be dancing, shaking herself to canned music blaring over the place. Letty would be along and say, "You remember my sister. She's back." Michele would look out from under that haircut with needy, lonesome eyes melting Aaron's fine heart. The familiar smell of aftershave wafted over Mary Virginia and all else she knew about him so well. "Come to my house," Michele would have said. "I can teach you to dance," responding to Aaron's compliments, to his downgrading himself. As taught? Mary Virginia thought.

Wives of the men who met for coffee would have known behind her back because once Aaron was missing, the others would have found out why. "Aaron's off again with that woman he's took up with." She heard the words in her head, the way they talked. And she was home, running the vacuum in a solitude she longed for. Jesus! Mary Virginia let herself think. So that coming from that house, wilted, spent, tremulous, still excited, who knows what, Aaron could have run straight through a stop sign with kudzu hung over it, into the path of a car with ten people in it, without even knowing. That foggy morning she remembered so well, he came home without his headlights on, having forgotten, the side-view mirror turned inward, where he would have seen a flash probably, something there and gone, quick like a silverfish. Slow, alone, intact in the middle of the highway, neither seeing right, nor hearing, with a neck too stiff to turn, Aaron would have gone on, and said later what he thought he guessed at but knew: A kid was driving, who could hardly see over the steering wheel. And she could not rat on her husband or prove anything either.

I am sore afraid, Mary Virginia thought, beginning to tremble. That woman would take him any way she could get him, any old safe port in a storm and a roof over her head. Aaron was after all a respected, elderly gentleman in the community. A catch, she suspected.

The photographer came in and Brad Richards after her, as close up behind as a hound sniffing a bitch's crack. His mouth formed, Oh no, when he saw Mary Virginia and he went back out. He rounded the tent and came in through an opposite flap. A shout came through a megaphone like a thunderclap, announcing the contest's winners. "Aaron Mortimer." A moment later, it was added, "And his missus, Mary Virginia."

People stopped dancing to congratulate him. The photographer stepped onto the platform, pulling the couple together, fixing Michele's hair, asking if she wanted more lipstick. The mistake was pointed out, and she turned with a sagging mouth toward the fat, frumpy housewife. There went her scoop before it ever got started, her cover story for *Parade* or *People* magazine, the rakish, cute gentleman in cat's whiskers, jitterbugging with the handsome, older woman, with an accompanying headline banner that shouted, Yes! There's Sex After Death. Mary Virginia thought suddenly she had missed something, something vital and important, and maybe life itself. Why, she thought, it's never been death I've been afraid of, it's been living. Aaron would go forward, and she would lapse. She had always been on the sidelines, nagging and complaining.

"Could you step up here, ma'm?" the photographer asked.

Mary Virginia started out. People who would have stopped, or aided her, could not. They were caught up in a crowd barging in. People wanted to hear the contest winners, to see Brad up closer, to get ice cream cards. She made her way outside where night was coming on. Fireflies darted everywhere and parking lights shone on cars. She went as fast as possible, bracing herself against the incline's tilt. Aaron kept car keys under the front seat, and she drove on past where kids had released the balloons. They soared overhead with the ominous silence of the Goodyear blimp. She forgot to turn on the air-conditioner and tears blew out a window.

As soon as she got home, Mary Virginia looked for shelter. She went through the silent, near-dark house into the bedroom and closet, seeking safety from tumult and thunder. She was huddled in a closet, hidden there beyond rows of clothes when car doors slammed and people began calling. There was a strangeness to having her name called all over the house by different voices. "She's got to be here. The car's outside."

They could be burglars stalking the house, rampaging, coming to steal while she cowered. The back yard was searched and people came back, tramping through the house. Inside they were still calling, closing in. They searched room by room, and Aaron said, "She couldn't be—" but there she was when he opened the door, throwing in light. A sneaker moved with a foot in it, and he called that out. "Mary Virginia," he said. "What on earth?"

"She's in there?" somebody asked.

"On the floor. Hiding in a corner," another person said. "Flipped her wig, I reckon."

Townspeople stared in, talking and asking what to do, wondering and speculating. "Call the Sheriff? The constable? Take her to the emergency room in Nashtoba?" "How you going to get her out?" someone asked. "She's heavy."

"Plumb off her rocker, that's for sure."

"They won't take them in the Sunset Rest Home like that. You got to go crazy after you get there."

"Only thing's the state asylum. Aaron's not some rich fellow who can afford a private place."

"He's saddled with it now."

"We've got to call somebody. We can't leave her here like this. They'll come tie you up if they have to."

A dampness between her legs turned into water; the spot beneath her grew larger. Mary Virginia sat on until hands began to lift her, reaching out from starched, white cuffs, smelling coolly and cleanly of antiseptics and medicines.

As she came free in the closet, words jarred loose in her chest. She suddenly knew the long-lost ones Aaron had not sung. *I love you, baby. But your feets too big.*

And he had not sung them. He said only, "Your feets too big." Now someone began to sing them in a faraway, but close-up voice. On and on, Mary Virginia rode away from home that night, hearing the singing, "I love you, baby," wondering where the voice came from.

Happy Anniversary

Tate McCall stared out from under the shade of his tree. Something tall and dark barreled toward him. Up close it turned into a man who said, "I'm sorry to wake you, Mr. Tate."

"You didn't wake me up. I'm not asleep."

"He's been asleep under that tree ten minutes." His wife, Allie, unlatched the door to the old lean-to back porch and looked out.

"I thought I heard someone catching z's." The man grinned.

"What can I do for you, young fellow?"

"I'm here to read the meter." The boy rapped his breast pocket with his flashlight, where stitching read either his name or that of his company. Tate couldn't make it out.

"The meter's over . . ."

"Have mercy, Tate. He knows where the meter is."

The boy stared at him as if expecting something to happen, but nothing did, so he continued, "I'm Rich Peters." One thing Tate knew, Rich Peters wasn't married. The boy went on, "My daddy's Gene. He says he knows you. He saw yours and Miss Allie's picture in the paper about your fiftieth anniversary. He thought that picture might have been taken a while back?"

"Twenty years ago," Tate said, smiling. "How is he?"

"Doing all right for . . ." and Rich Peters swallowed and said, "He's fine."

Doing all right for an old man, Tate thought. The fellow's feet went off, and Tate got up; he had to finish cutting his grass before that party tomorrow. The weather was so hot. He sat down a minute, his cap pulled low. I wasn't asleep, Tate told himself.

His stomach grumbled when it was only eleven o'clock. Maybe he ought to eat something: him in the kitchen by himself and Allie in the next room in front of her soap story. This time tomorrow the party would nearly be here. Tate looked toward it with dread and worry, and had to get his grass cut by then.

He set a brown-spotted hand on each knee. Their veins, dark and purple, jumped out, his blood always rushing to his thin skin's surface and staying there. He would not show any effort getting up; he meant to remain silent. The young man's feet loitered on the edge of his eyesight; he was no closer to the door where Allie stood, teetering on the sill, holding onto the door more than holding it open. After her recent hip replacement she didn't seem to be doing better. She was still on a cane, still hobbling about, still making soft little cries when she got up. He wondered if they were not two pitiful people batting around the house, Allie sometimes barking orders like she was Lord and Master when what she was was a crippled-up old woman with a tendency toward being right.

They might not be so old, seventy-five years each. But they'd had some bad luck about health. Some nights, lying awake, Tate prayed neither of them would have a stroke.

His arteries were corroded and could not be cleaned out again—he'd had triple bypass surgery. His doctor in Memphis said he might not come out of any more anesthetic; he could not risk going under any more knives. "Mr. McCall's a walking miracle," the doctor said. One time he said, "He doesn't get enough oxygen to the brain, you know," speaking in a low tone and thinking Tate could not overhear him. Allie was all the time telling people, "Tate's getting so he can't hear thunder," when she was the one going deaf. Tate could see her in his mind's eye this minute, head cocked, eyes looking inward, and finally admitting to the other fellow what she had to admit to herself, "I didn't hear what you said." While Tate, if he didn't hear something, didn't let on about it. Most folks didn't say much worth hearing anyway, was his estimate. He walked away letting folks wonder if he heard or not.

The boy's feet were coming back. "Can I help you up?" he said, Rich something-or-other. The young man was about to grab hold of him like somebody trying to help a hurt bird by one wing. Tate clutched his arms to himself, said, "I can do it," and added, "Thanks."

He remembered the name "Gene" had come up, and he used to know a Gene Peters in Nashtoba: might be the boy's daddy; probably was. With his spotted hands on khaki knees, Tate stood up. For a minute, bolts of red, blue, and violet shot through his eyes. When his sight cleared, he said, "I've got to cut this grass."

"It's mighty hot work for a day like this."

The boy stood directly in front of the sun again, a dark shadow, blotting it out the way he had before.

"Tate, don't cut any more grass in this heat," Allie called. "You've done enough."

She was probably right, he thought. Drat it. The door swung out as she spoke, and if it swung any farther, Allie was going to fly straight into the air, like a chicken let out of a coop. She didn't have her cane with her, was practicing walking around the house without it. "You should have started days earlier if you wanted all this cut by tomorrow," she said.

Tate said nothing, and the boy pretended not to have heard her. "Can't somebody do it for him?" he asked.

Tate shook his fist, thinking *I can do it myself!* "You can't get anybody in the country to do any work," Allie said. "They're all on some kind of check."

"My mother says white people are taking up the slack. She's got white women coming to clean house."

"You don't mean to tell me. That hasn't happened in the country, not yet," Allie said. "I guess it will, though. Everything else has changed."

She started shoving the door closed over a warped wooden floor, shutting herself and that boy into what Tate considered his private world, the quiet back porch, sealed against the weather with plastic sheeting when it used to stand open and screened-in. Being in it was like being in a storm cloud, troubled, gray, and nearly airless. And what was she doing in it? Probably she was out there just to let the boy in, or to rummage around in that freezer of hers for the party tomorrow.

That freezer was stocked up against some rainy day in the next century. In their two lifetimes they would never eat up what-all was in there, he told her. They would lose thousands of dollars' worth of food if the power went out, or the box went bust. Sometimes he thought of fooling with the coils himself just to prove he could be right.

Was she getting ready for that party tomorrow? Who was coming? Their nieces and nephews giving the party put a write-up in the county paper, *The Democrat*, saying "Friends and Family Are Invited." "Might be two folks show up, might be two hundred," somebody commented. Shoot, Tate thought. He didn't know two hundred folks alive any longer.

He went toward the tractor, smelling his cut grass. He stopped outside the sheeting, where two shadows were etched, and thought maybe Allie had that freezer stocked up to prove something: if a woman had that much food left over, she had to have been living, didn't she? She was telling the boy, "All he's got left to do is cut grass. And go to White-hill twice a day to meet men for coffee. I dread the day the doctor says he can't drive. He'll have to tell him. I couldn't."

"I thought Mr. Tate used to have some cows?"

"He couldn't take care of them. Had to give them up spring before last."

My foot, Tate thought. She was as bad off as he was. Maybe worse. Allie's greatest fear was she'd go before he did. He heard her tell folks, "Tate can't live by himself. He never has, and never will." He let her go on thinking he was deafer than he was because that way he heard a lot.

He had gone straight from his mother's house into the army and then, on one weekend leave, into getting married. What had been the hurry? The war; that's what. Everything had been speeded up. There was not going to be any tomorrow. That was what all the songs, the sermons, the talk, and the picture shows said. If only he'd known . . . there had been a million tomorrows.

He thought about standing before the Baptist preacher with a license he and Allie rushed over to Nashtoba and got so quick the ink might not have been dry. Maybe it wasn't legal. Tate scratched under his cap brim now, wondering. *Fif*-ty years, he told himself in a solemn manner, measured and nearly funereal.

Back then he had been a free agent except for the army and his mother telling him what to do. The next minute there had been all this fiddling among the womenfolk just like for this party tomorrow, and he had been caught up in it—till now he felt he ought to shout out to somebody, Watch out, Brother!

Suddenly his heart hurt—unwarranted; unexpected. Just the way the doctor told him it could happen. The place in his chest felt like a panic button. He wanted to cry out for help. He could not imagine an empty half of bed without Allie when they had slept together in one for so long, he on his side and she on hers.

Sometimes the cat, Miss Kitty, slept in the bed with them. Under guise of being a tame calico, she was a wild creature. He thought of her eyes in the dark, lightening and darkening, signaling something. When she was in bed between them, it was nice having something soft, cozy, furry down in that hollow. He would never be able to endure the house by himself, sit before TV daily and nightly the way they did now, though he was not that interested, without Allie's explanations and her guessing aloud before the contestants' answers to "Wheel of Fortune" or "Jeopardy."

What was his alternative? The Sunset Rest Home over in Nashtoba, where there were bars on the windows and folks in white uniforms tied you into chairs with bedsheets. He'd been over there visiting folks who didn't have any more idea than a jackrabbit who he was, or themselves, either, in their damp diapers.

Allie's shadow crossed the plastic toward another room. He could not let himself be caught malingering, standing empty-handed, because under such circumstances Allie always looked at him queerly, asking, What are you doing, Tate? He never found voice to answer, Thinking, woman.

Tate hiked off, jealous about his porch. Time had passed, and he had given up farming, then his cattle. He took up a little housekeeping to spare Allie and her arthritis on days the cleaning girl didn't come, *A man's got to do something!* Now part of his daily experience was sweeping up after Kitty McCall. The cat had come to the door unbidden one day, mewling and crying—and Tate opened it to her widely, saying, "You found us, did you?" his heart widening too in love and affection and the need to take care of something.

He swept up cat hairs, clumps, from wherever Puss landed on her soft feet. Those hairs, crumbs, the dust that came from nowhere, the strange debris of living, formed satisfactory piles in front of his toes before he swept them into a dustpan. Then he washed his and Allie's few minor dishes. They never did talk about a division of chores; things just evolved. He made up his side of the bed, and she made up hers.

Out on the porch were the washer and dryer. Going around the house, it was easy for him to pick up Allie's slip on a chair, her nightgown not hung up, his wash-and-wear shirt on a doorknob, underdrawers where he stepped out of them. Tate liked watching the soap powder pour in, the blue, eddying swirl that carried him to some distant thought of Niagara Falls. He had always believed he would go there someday with whomever he married. Probably because as a boy he collected tinted postcards with pictures of places. That was how he went somewhere, too, looking at scenes scattered in his boyhood drawer. He liked the dependability of cycles, the recurring WASH RINSE HOLD, and afterwards the dryer steaming up the plastic with drops of moisture like rain or tears.

"Tate," Allie would say from her lounger, pained legs up, "there's no human reason to wash every day for two people. And leave my things alone. You've ruint enough putting them in the dryer when they're not supposed to go."

Allie stayed busy as a hornets' nest making things for a crafts fair. All year she painted, crocheted, sewed, made tiny, glittery Christmas trees and hair ornaments from fish scales, painted in the right season to look like poinsettias. She made tie tacks and lapel pins from the tiniest unopened cotton bolls, which they collected in the fall. She was creative, she was good! She outsold everybody. Allie said in a later lifetime she'd have been a business person up in Memphis, with a shop, instead of a housekeeper with no housekeeping left to do.

Round a corner of the house, Tate saw a tractor tire going flat. Kneeling to inspect it, he had another worry: Could he get back up? The nieces and nephews told Allie not to do anything about this party; she was one-half of its honored guests. Yet here came another of the nieces up the driveway, spattering gravel, to borrow something else. Ruthie got out of her car, saying, "I came to see if Aunt Allie's got a big ice tea pitcher. And some punch cups."

After a few puzzled seconds, she said, "Can I help you up?" Since Tate frequently said nothing, she did not wait long for an answer. "Aren't you excited? Aunt Allie says she's thrilled to death about tomorrow. It's her most exciting day, I guess. That is, except for getting married!" Ruthie went on cozily toward the house. A cateress was doing the party but everybody was pitching in.

Cateress? Tate thought. It sounded like a party too fancy for him. Maybe the party would be the biggest excitement Allie'd had since— well, since getting married, the way she had wanted to do. He looked back over that fuzzy wartime experience, the wedding and honeymoon, all two nights' worth of it. 1942; Lord help us, Tate said to himself.

The first night in Memphis he thought Allie was going to bleed to death, worse than any stuck pig he'd ever seen. She told him, "At least you know you got a virgin." He did not tell her that didn't make a fig's worth of difference to him. Nookey was nookey no matter how you looked at it.

The second night one of his brothers arrived, having driven all the way from Nashtoba to carry him to the ball game. "Just arrived?" Allie gasped when Sheldon phoned up from the Peabody's lobby. Sheldon thought they were yokels who didn't know what to do in a city for a night, Allie said. Tate remembered that what he'd had in mind was taken care of by that box of Kotex on the toilet tank. When Allie said she soaked a pad before she could get it on good, that was not information he wanted to know about his bride. He was excited about seeing the Memphis Chicks play; they had a one-armed fellow on the team. He could no longer remember the man's name.

But Tate recalled Allie in the stands with her wedding corsage quivering, lips set, arms folded, and madder than forty wet hens through an extra inning. Allie said she never was hick enough to wear a corsage to a ball game. Maybe she had been mad ever since? Tate stuck a blade of grass in his mouth to think about that.

They made him a mess sergeant down at Camp Shelby. There was nothing you could tell the Army; they told you. Just because he was a Mississippi country boy didn't mean he knew how to boil water. He didn't. And his mother might have been a Mississippi widow-lady, but black folks did all her work. Country biscuits appeared on the table every morning along with fresh churned butter, which might be why his arteries corroded. There was fried quail, home-cured pork, sausage, bacon, and country ham so salty you drank a gallon of sweetmilk to get over it. There he was one morning, twelve years old, sopping up redeye gravy with biscuits when his father, opposite, put down a greased chin toward a belly he couldn't button his shirt over. "Run quick. Get Dr. Crowley," screamed the Negro woman working for them at the time, old Stella. His mother was in bed, where she stayed mostly those years.

Tate could hear again the *whoosh* of corduroy knickers rubbing as he made tracks down the road. He had bolted straight into the man's kitchen, where the doctor was eating, too, and shouted, "It's Poppa." Dr. Crowley got up and had them back down that dust-track road in his Ford in two minutes. Spirits rose up off these country roads, they'd walk with you too, and Dr. Crowley in spirit told him again, "Son, your Daddy has passed. Bless this house. Now you're head of it."

But that had not happened. His mother got out of the sickbed, brushed her night table clear of Lydia Pinkham's and the other female remedies of the time, laced with morphine. Many of the ladies went around with sweet, smiling, agreeable dispositions from drinking enough syrup. Arvenia McCall never had another sick minute till she died of a stroke in her late eighties. She grew more strong-minded. When professional ball scouts came around looking over boys playing in their leagues in pastures, one of them tapped Tate. He would have had to go to St. Louis. His mother put her foot down.

Rich Peters, stalking up behind him, said, "Your tire's going flat, Mr. Tate."

"I can see it is, young man."

"Maybe Miss Allie's right. You've cut enough. You've done the front, and that's all folks will see. Isn't the party down at the Community Center?"

Tate said, "Yes," staring over his toes at his grass, at the road through town, to a building where a black sign read "Itna Homa Volunteer Fire Department." The fire truck sat in a shed where coats and boots were stored. The main building was available for anybody's function. Thirty or so years ago when the fire department started, Tate had been one of its first volunteers.

"Playing firemen," the womenfolk teased the men, while taking perfectly seriously their jobs' importance. When the signal went out, as if over the universe, *Ugh Ugh Ugh* like a cough, hearts rose into throats. Tate remembered some of the old excitement. He said to Rich Peters, "I wanted to get my grass cut."

Tate considered the tractor an old friend, and he was afraid he and it would play out: Give up the ghost, he often said. He did not want to buy another even if this one was on its last, limping leg, the way he was. Running it was fun. Chance. He never knew if it was going to start or stop. He depended on the tractor now to help him get back up. Once the boy was gone, he would grab hold of it and hoist. He said, "Son, you don't know what somebody's going to see. Or do, either. Folks have been running in and out of here for weeks. Folks we haven't seen in a hundred years are liable to turn up tomorrow, come up here to see how we live and what we've got." Go away talking behind our backs, too; he knew that much. He was liable not to know anybody.

Maybe he could get out of going? Play sick. Play dead. He would complain of a headache, a bellyache, a pain in his new heart, or stick a finger down his throat and vomit. They would drag him there anyhow, and he knew it. They would send an ambulance, carry him on a stretcher, feet first in and feet first out, the way he was going out soon. He had to attend the party because he was one-half of its honored guests. Married fifty years.

He hated for the meter man to see his faded, dented truck. It was parked under the shade of an elm. Worn out like the rest of us, Tate thought. It wasn't that he couldn't buy a new truck; he could. But he was tired of replacing the old with the new, clogged arteries with cleaned-out ones, a true heart with one of plastic, a hip of bone with one of metal. Nothing seemed real anymore. Sometimes at night, he thought he heard Allie's new hip clanking beside him. Before she got it, the old one sounded as if it needed oil.

Ruthie and Allie came out. "Tate," Allie said, "don't stay out here getting heatstroke, you hear?" Then she turned whiter than a sheet.

"My hydrangeas," she cried, putting her hands over her face. Tate could not help thinking, Peek-a-boo. But this was serious. "Why did you prune them to the very ground?" she asked. Allie's eyes shone the color of little wild violets in the grass in summertime. She turned to Ruthie. "Men will always do it when they don't have something else to do. Just prune prune prune. Cut cut cut. Those bushes are ruint. They'll never flower again in my lifetime."

Under his cap brim Tate said to himself, Ruined. He wondered where Allie got the word's misuse when, having taught school, she prided herself on knowing more than the next fellow. Every morning she worked the crossword puzzle in the Memphis paper till each block was covered. She had a lot of dictionaries: Latin, French, German, he didn't know what-all. Still, when she didn't know something, Allie was not embarrassed to ask. Tate admired her for that. She got the same look as when she didn't hear, head cocked, eyes indrawn, that questioning, thinking look of a bird. She always had to ask him sports questions. What's the name of the home run king, Babe . . .? Anybody would know that, but sometimes he wouldn't be able to think. Who was the Say Hey Kid? It was not, he'd think, Mickey Mantle. By the time he remembered, yesterday's paper would be in the trash. It would seem to Tate he had to go a long way back in time to remember. Legendary figures, events, faded into somebody else's experience, not his own. His own lifetime seemed to be still ahead, peopled with figures and events yet to come.

Ruthie got in her car with her arms loaded and spattered back down the driveway. "Well," she had said, looking like a scared pet rabbit. Tate was her uncle, but Allie was clearly in the right about those flowers. "See you tomorrow," Ruthie said, and flew away to the silent emptiness of the countryside.

Allie said, "Well," too, stricken and resigned. Tate smirked under his cap brim, thinking of another child's rejoinder: "Well's a deep hole in the ground." Allie went inside to the allure of whatever soap story was on. The meter man pretended not to see those bushes either, and Tate, his face shaded, peeking, thought they did look mighty low to the ground: mighty. Like overgrown mushrooms. He did not remember clipping so much as he remembered a sense of satisfaction about going around and around, a feeling of completion, that you started on one side and met yourself on the other. He remembered from another lost time the sound of horses' hooves, the way now he faintly remembered the click of shears.

Rich Peters needed to be off. He looked as if he wanted to say something. But he was only a service person, paid to come here and paid to go. His conversations with customers were usually about the weather. "It's faired up nicely," he said. "You'll have a pretty day tomorrow."

Tate looked up. Wind from the south would bring good weather, though hotter. He stared in the same direction as Rich Peters, seeing the light company's yellow truck on the road. "I wondered how you . . ."

"I checked the meter at the store and walked here." Tate thought back to the time he'd walk in this heat when he didn't have to.

A car stopped at the Center unloading what seemed to be a bunch of girls, women anyhow. They rushed around measuring the handicap ramp's railings. No telling what they were up to about that party. Several of them hung flower baskets from hooks on the porch's ceiling. Tate wanted to cry, Watch out! There were wasps in the eaves. He wanted to feel needed and necessary and even that he was a savior.

Rich said, "What's happened to this community? There used to be four stores here when I started, and now there's one."

"Shoot," Tate told him. "When I was a boy there were seven stores. A hotel. Business college. Boardinghouse."

"You're kidding." Rich whistled. Tate went on telling all the things that used to be on the road through town, and liked how the boy's eyes widened. There was a blacksmith's shop, and an old store where somebody—one of his brothers actually—used to show picture shows on Saturday nights. "A nickel to get in. Tom Mix shoot-'em-ups." Tate cocked an ever-ready trigger finger. There used to be a town pump in a gazebo where folks swapped gossip and watered horses. A cotton gin. Feed store. Awe deepened on the young man's face about the passage of time, the way Tate wanted.

He went on in a smooth voice once compared to Bing Crosby's, mellow and low. Even singing church music, which was all Tate sang in public, he had a crooning, lovelorn quality he could not help. He was singing for the love of Jesus, townfolks liked to comment. No one died but that Tate was asked to sing at the funeral. Baptist or Methodist—for once denomination was forgotten. Now, though, his voice had lost its timbre and fiber. It had a lonesome sound like the far-off reed of a piper. He could no longer keep on key and had given up singing aloud even in the shower, where he used to try to tempt Allie to wash alongside him. "Go on, boy," she would say, blushing. She never could get over her strict, Baptist, country-girl's upbringing. Or could she? Tate wondered.

"I haven't been in that store since Loma Murphy died," he said, looking over his knees at the one remaining store. "And those new folks bought it. Everybody shops now in supermarkets, like Allie. Makes stuff too expensive to tote it out to the country. Those new folks are liable to get nickeled and dimed to death." What, he thought, would happen to the main road through town with everything emptying out?

Loma Murphy, Tate said, would do a turnaround in her grave, if she hadn't already, about what had been done to her store. She'd kept it the way it was built in the 1860s and with its own sense of worth and dignity. Now these new folks had it covered up with siding. Allie mourned from the front window the day that happened, "This whole countryside's going to be nothing but aluminum." They also mourned the old churches, their two in town, covered over. Every day they had to fight salesmen coming to their door wanting to cover their house the same way.

Tate had heard that in Loma's store there were glass-fronted refrigerated cases big enough to stand in, lit by neon. At night they shone out to the road like the fierce, anxious, red eyes of foxes. Loma had only one small case, the meat growing ever more rancid as folks started driving elsewhere to shop. She had a single butcher block to cut up cheese and chickens. You always did get, Tate said, a feather along with your Velveeta.

But he wouldn't tell stories any longer. Pretty soon Rich would get that slack-jawed look young people got when you went on too long about the past. Someday Rich Peters might mention not being able to go to the moon for a day's shopping or say once the government ran the whole business, and he'd get back those same looks. Rich said, "I guess you've seen a lot of changes," his flashlight hanging from one hand.

He looked so sweet, so innocent, so young, Tate wanted to hug him to his breast, be his mother and father both. He had no children. Only lately had he begun to feel that lack. Why the situation existed neither he nor Allie nor any doctor could ever figure out. He and Allie concluded, It is God's will. But what had God's will meant?

Tate told Rich about Loma Murphy's writing her name in script in wet cement on her store porch, with a finely whittled willow stick a colored boy fixed her. She wrote so carefully, her tongue between her teeth, that in recounting, Tate sensed her saying the letters slowly, one by one, *L* and *O* . . . The old men playing checkers on her porch got off their kegs to watch. Loma never married and had no children, and that was what she left, he supposed, her name in concrete.

Feet crossed that name daily, few of their owners knowing now who Loma was or why her name was there. She seemed not even to be past history. Tate thought he could not tell this boy the truth. He could never say, Look at me. See the future. Didn't the boy see it already? He wouldn't tell the boy about hidden things, like leaking in your britches before you made it to the bathroom.

Tate said, "I've lived here all my life except for my time in the war."

"What war would that be?" Rich asked.

Tate looked at his watch crystal as if to provide himself an answer. "The Second World War, son," he answered.

Rich was obviously embarrassed. "Of course," he said. Mr. Tate was not so old he could have been in any war before that. Rich repeated, "Lived here all your life. Not many folks can say that any longer. About growing where you are planted." He looked away at the grass recently cut, at the sky and the trees and the main road. The wonder that dawned this time was not what Tate intended.

He pointed past Dr. Crowley's old home, saying, "Down that road's where I came from," and looked back at the house, which had been Allie's widowed Daddy's. Maybe that was another mistake, living in someone else's castle with no say-so of your own. He had a foreboding that years hence he'd be wandering this place, a ghostly ghost, without anybody's knowing he'd been here in the first place. The same house would be on the same hill, with the pasture and the pond, while the hydrangea bushes would have sprung back and flowered.

Rich Peters made his way off, wishing Tate good luck on the party tomorrow. Halfway down the slope he turned back, saying, "Can I help with that tire?"

Tate waved him on. Good-bye; good luck, he meant. He thought he could do it. Otherwise he would have to go after Preacher Allan to help. Preacher was an old black man who'd retired about the time Tate had. They'd been friends since the beginning, when they rode bareback on horses, using rope for a bridle. Now they rode in Tate's truck, covering the same territory. Tate grabbed the tractor to hoist himself and let out a yelp of pain.

Kitty McCall, sleeping on the truck's cab, awoke. Her eyes might have been shut, she may have been asleep, but she knew the movement of every mouse in the pasture. In yellow evenings, when willows met in the pond, she battled minnows at the water's edge with one paw. Many nights from his doorway, Tate stood calling, "Here, Puss," and she never came inside. She was the cat who walked by herself. As much as he envied her freedom, Tate envied her courage more. Kitty McCall was neutered, and no protectorate waited for her in the night. She went off to meet nobody, and nobody looked for her. She strayed into the dark, alone, heeding what called her.

He set to work with the tire iron after a hard trek to get it. Bolts of color shot through his eyes. Then he saw everything as he thought Rich Peters must have seen it. He prodded and pried a long time; at last the tire iron had things moving. Then, as he tried to lift the flat, the jack flew back and hit him in the head.

Tate was stunned. A biblical phrase formed in his mind: Why hast thou forsaken me? A melancholy overtook him. The next minute he would have returned the truck a swift kick. But a curtain of blood streamed before his eyes. He saw his shirt was covered with it. He was afraid to touch his forehead, knowing the cut to be wide. One half-inch lower and the jack would have gouged out his eye. He groped his way to the house.

Allie, inside, must have heard fumbling at the door. "Tate!" she screamed. She took him to a bathroom where he leaned close, taking in her warmth and scent of toilet water, soap; he smelled antiseptic, felt her soft fingers, and remembered his mother, Vicks salve, sassafras tea, mustard plasters, and old Stella.

Allie, applying a wing-shaped Band-Aid, crimped the edges closed. She wanted to call someone to carry him to the doctor in Whitehill or the emergency room at Nashtoba. He might need stitches. He would only have a little headache, Tate said, smiling weakly, and he took his second aspirin of the day (he took one every morning for his heart). At noon he ate some pot roast and potatoes in the kitchen and then went to lie on a sofa in the room where Allie sat for his near-about-all-day nap.

Tate got up to eat supper before going back to sleep. Allie, as she often did, said, "How can you sleep so much?" At nine Tate liked to get up from his after-supper nap to go to bed. Allie always stayed up for the ten o'clock news. "How can you sleep so much?" she said. "Can you hand me the little box please for changing channels?"

Here came the windup! Here came the pitch! Just like in the good old days of baseball. The black box sailed across the room. Allie caught it on the fly, smartly, an old tomboy herself. "Why, boy," she said. "What on earth?"

Tate turned with a slight grin, not really knowing what he had expected. Allie told people he slept through the night and she stayed awake. But plenty nights he heard her snoring, and the creaking of trees, noise that might be Miss Puss wanting in or was merely the sound that came with ruminations of the past.

Tonight Allie bustled around in her kitchen later than usual doing something for that party, and happy, happy as a lark.

The next day, having studied his Sunday school lesson, Tate was going off to church. Allie had not started back since her operation. Holding his book, he lingered in the door. Maybe she needed him to come home after Sunday school? "Do what you want to do," Allie told him. She was busy with her box of fish scales. She had not started back either to the beauty shop in Mabel Wilkins's house; the steps were too high. This morning Mabel was coming to do Allie's hair at home. "Don't tell anybody," she said. "I only do this on special occasions"— like for a death, she meant. "But this is special."

Turning from the door, Tate went up as close as possible to Allie, clinging to his Sunday school book, and asked, "Are you going to change my Band-Aid?" Allie put her box down slowly. She shoved aside a cup of decaf; old folks had to give up caffeine too. She stood up with a full light of understanding in her eyes. She was a mother at last. Fifty years late, she might have been saying to herself. They stood together at the medicine chest mirror, eyes never meeting.

Tate drove away thinking *she* was the one crippled-up, but he got the shocked looks: the I-haven't-seen-Tate-in-so-long-doesn't-he-look-awful looks. So old; like a cadaver. Just like his Momma in her last years, people said.

In Sunday school he was called on to interpret the lesson. He did not want to talk in church any longer. "I've talked here enough," Tate said. "Let the young people do it." They rule the earth, he thought. Asked to pass the collection plate, he did not want to walk up and down the aisles any longer either. When he walked up and down, people seemed to want him to say something, but he did not know what they wanted to hear.

Allie kept at him about his missing bottom teeth. "You look like this," she said, sticking out her lip, wagging her chin up and down. "Like you're chewing a cud." He looked like those old men at Luma's store, she said, who used to spit tobacco toward the road and hit their galluses.

When he came home, the house smelled like a beauty parlor, of Clorox or chloroform. There had never been a time in his life when he thought, This is my house: because it was Allie's. It would be hers long after her death. The old man left things so bollixed up that nobody would ever get clear title. He'd added codicil after codicil trying to make things come out right in the hereafter. If Allie died and Tate remarried, no wife of his or her prior issue could inherit house or land. No issue he might have with another woman could inherit anything. All he knew was, the old man could have saved himself a lot of time, effort, and money into a lawyer's pocket. Remarry? Whoo, boy, he thought.

He did not have time to put away his Bible before Allie started in on him. "Tate," she said as he came in, "when did you put this in the dryer? I thought I had my good things hidden." She held up something about the size Kitty McCall might wear. With a sob Allie said it was her camisole. "The lace was real. It went with the suit I was going to wear." Clearly, Tate didn't know what she was talking about, and she quit explaining. Allie rummaged through drawers, saying she did not have anything else to put on. Pretty soon, nieces swarmed in going cluck-cluck. They passed Tate, who was trying to eat chicken pot pie for noon dinner and acting, manlike, as if he did not know what the ruckus was about. They carried on in the bedroom like a bunch of kids till he reminded himself those nieces were middle-aged, with lined faces. With Mabel gone, they styled and restyled Allie's hair. "We don't want it set-looking," one of them said. "Mabel's still into too many little curls."

"I don't want it teased," Allie said.

"No. We want it just like this—whuff!"

Allie came out looking like a new person. Tate said, "You look pretty."

They all came back through the kitchen. One of the nieces followed Allie like a bridal attendant, straightening her hem. Another ran behind, fastening her necklace. Tate muttered, "I see you found something else to wear"; but he said that into his plate, and no one heard. It was a joke nobody would think was funny. Everybody still wore grim reminders around their eyes about the dryer incident.

A niece said, "Here's Merle Norman's newest shade, Aunt Allie. Purple Passion. Try that on." They all gathered around, giggling, at a mirror while Allie applied the lipstick. Following the nieces out, Allie said, "I may burn up in this suit even if it's cotton. But old ladies have got to cover their arms." Tate wanted to take a nap. The others finally departed, unsettling his gravel and kicking up dust.

"What happened to your hydrangeas?" one of the nieces asked.

"Oh, you know." Allie gave a throaty laugh and an explanation he could not hear. You might as well be philosophical, he thought, lying down. *What's done is done. No sense crying over spilt milk.* He fell asleep.

Allie told him later, "It's time, Tate." He rose quickly, defensively, as if to meet a challenge, a dare, some fellow who wanted to fight, and wondered what he had been dreaming about. Having showered and shaved that morning, he had only to put back on his suit. He'd left it stretched across the bed with its arms out to keep from wrinkling. Now it was gone—put away, he suspected, by one of the nieces. He had to search for it.

Allie did not mention walking to the Center, though it was only a few feet, and downhill. She would not let him drive her Chevrolet, and he did not want to. Its seatbelt ran back of its own accord and held him by the throat as if to choke him. The dashboard lit up like a circus. There were cars these days that actually spoke, told you, Put on your seatbelt. Don't stand too close. Good Lord, Tate thought. He was still longing for the days of Dr. Crowley's old Ford with its horn going Ah-ooga, Ah-ooga.

Tate wondered when the doctor would stop his driving. That happening was as inevitable as death and taxes. There were few places to pass in the hills, and maybe he was a menace, driving slowly because of his poor reflexes. A line of cars congregated in his rearview mirror. Drivers were probably gritting their teeth. At the worst possible moments, they flew around him on curves as if they could not stand crawling another minute. He feared causing an accident.

Allie parked at the side of the building, leaving space in front for guests. In its shed, the fire truck seemed to grin in self-importance. The door was always left open in case of a hasty departure. Good day, Tate bade it in silence.

Allie went ahead of him on her cane. The handicap ramp's railings were wrapped with gold crepe paper. He guessed yellow balloons were the closest thing to golden. They were filled with helium, tied on; they rose up like a bunch of bald-headed fellows. It was going to be hot inside that place too, he'd betcha. The ramp was easier than managing steps, Allie said. Just then one of those faceless, yellow, bald-headed fellows popped in the heat all by itself. "He'p my soul," Allie cried. "I thought I was shot."

"I hope everybody doesn't crowd in on time," Tate warned. "It's going to be hot inside."

"There isn't any set time, Tate," Allie said. "It's open house from four to six."

"There you got it, fellow." A countryman slapped Tate on the back, giving him a broad wink. "You and me ought to be out of here fishing," the man said.

Tate dropped back slowly behind others. He finally went into a room with window air-conditioners and ceiling fans trying to distribute air. Baskets of bronze and yellow flowers were everywhere. People were already sneezing, and he'd be next; everything might be gold in honor, but goldenrod had been mixed in by mistake. Children had picked it by the roadsides, and his heart went out to all who helped. Mabel sat at a table with an autograph book. Tate bent down until Allie spoke. "You don't have to sign your name, Tate. We know you're here."

"Have mercy," she said to others, with a joshing look to gloss over another of his mistakes. Mabel laughed along behind her hand. Another man slapped him on the back. "This party's for womenfolks, Tate. What do you think?" the townsman asked, going past.

Tate took a golden gumdrop from a dish, though without his bottom teeth, he could never chew it. The thought of crusty sugar made his gums ache. "Can't you see yourself in a mirror?" Allie would ask. "See how you look? Just you wait. Some Friday evening when we're eating at Roy Rogers' in Nashtoba, I'm not going to wear my bottom teeth. See if you're not embarrassed." But as often as she threatened, Allie never left home without her chompers. Tate thought about the day he had his teeth fitted. The dentist kept him in the chair so long that his ankles swelled and his toes went to sleep. The chair gripped his head so long, he heard music from outer space. The man's knuckles had kept pressing the roof of his mouth toward his skull, and he could not cry out. The dentist's hands were slicked up in rubber gloves as if he knew to be careful of this particular patient—Tate McCall—who was one big known germ carrier. He got up finally, saying, "They fit," and walked out. He hid the bottom teeth at home and had not seen them since; they hurt.

There's been enough waiting in life, Tate thought. Now, with the pen in his hand, and the autograph book unsigned, he wondered, What have I been waiting for? The answer came back to him purely and simply, For death.

Next to the autograph book was a picture in a gold frame of a handsome young couple. It seemed to have been taken in the present because the girl's skirt was up to her knees. She was tall and thin and bent at the waist toward the young man. His army cap was pushed back at a rakish angle, and he grinned underneath brazenly, straight at the camera. That's us, Tate thought, with a jolt. He could hardly believe it. "Isn't it a shame what happens to people," Allie muttered. To others she said loudly, "That was taken right after the ceremony. On a day as hot as this."

"I 'member it so good," an old lady said. "Tate looked like he could eat you up with a spoon."

"I remember his rushing her off after that license," a man said. "Afraid she'd get away from him."

"He wouldn't give her one minute," a woman laughed.

"I had a rip in the underarm of my dress. And Tate wouldn't let me stop to change," Allie said.

"Allie wore her corsage to a ball game," Tate said. "The next evening." Nobody heard. Nobody ever listened to a bridegroom, he guessed. Once you were a bride it seemed you always were one. Making his way through a bevy of people, he tried to put together names with faces. There seemed to be so many old folks in the room, and he wondered, Do I look as old as them? Some of the women had a blue tint to their hair, and some had a rose hue he thought must be a mistake on Mabel's part. In this room were the only people he'd known all his life who were still left living. People standing around patted themselves on the back about that. It seemed to be the accomplishment of their lives, that they were living.

Tate was the last of seven brothers and sisters. How'd he feel about outlasting everybody? somebody asked. He did not answer. How did they think he felt? What is wrong with people that they could ask a question so stupid? Couldn't they imagine for themselves, feel it even, what it was like in these blue-shaded hills once peopled with his people, to have them all gone?

They moved ahead of him everywhere. A brother, Ralph, hailed him in the distance with a brace of quail, all of them covertly clad, hidden in brown. The youngest sister, Flossie, who was home only a short time while he was, had learned to drive Poppa's car and scooted ahead of him in it, still. He had come a long time after the others; his mother was nearly fifty when he was born. The last thing on earth she must have wanted was another baby.

Maybe that was why she took to her bed. Maybe that was why Poppa ate himself so corpulent he could hardly ride a horse. Yet wasn't he a comfort to his mother once she was widowed? He went back to that September morning when he was in his knickers and Poppa suddenly put down his chin toward a big belly, leaving forever alone in a kitchen a startled boy and an old woman.

At the time Poppa was chewing his favorite food, gristle. We didn't know not to eat fat or red meat, Tate said to himself. He passed up that minute a bowl of salted nuts and some butter-rich cookies the ladies had busted their bustles making golden. Taking care of himself the way he was, he could live to be as old as Methuselah—older; who needed that?

Everywhere were bowls of white-chocolate mints, smaller than quarters and emblazoned with the numeral 50. He took one nut. One goober couldn't hurt anybody. Gumming it, he thought about the monkeyshines his parents had been up to at near his age. He thought how all that left him so much earlier. A doctor had agreed when asked that the medicines Mr. McCall was taking for his surgeries, his heart condition, for high blood pressure could lead to—and what had the fellow said? A loss of libido. Tate smiled in the present as he had smiled in the past, wondering why the man couldn't have put it so much more simply. If he told the gospel truth, he had not missed that activity so much. He did not believe Allie had either. Maybe he never had been a sexy person. There was nobody to ask; his wife had no basis for comparison.

He stopped. Allie said, "Here's the punch table. Doesn't it look pretty?"

Ruthie poured more ginger ale over a mound of lemon sherbet, saying, "I'm trying to make it look golden."

"Maybe you should have used orange sherbet, hon."

"Oh, Aunt Allie. Of course I should have. You're right."

Tate, after downing a cup of the stuff, didn't believe color would make any difference. It was not as cold as you wanted something in this weather either. He wanted to loosen his tie but was afraid of ruffling Allie's feathers. When another balloon popped outside, she grabbed herself, crying, "My soul!"

Gold streamers blew away from window units and tickled his face. He and Allie were too crowded, sitting as they were told to at one end of the room, like royalty. People kept coming up and offering congratulations. Some brought presents, though *The Democrat*'s write-up clearly said not to. What on earth could be in all those boxes for two old folks who needed nothing? Allie sighed beside him.

His underdrawers grew damp. Her face powder streaked and slid down her cheeks like sad, slow-moving wrinkles. If he did have to tell the truth, part of his interest in the activity went away because he got tired of climbing on an aging woman, who eventually was heftier than he was.

People, coming up, talked about the exploits of his brothers and sisters. "I remember Herbert," a man said, "nearly burning down this community smoking behind the feed store when he wasn't but seven."

"Four stores went," another person added.

"I recall James catching that near-'bout-hundred-pound catfish in Grey Wolf River," a man told.

"I remember your sister Katie eloping. My land! That was so romantic. Just like in storybooks." Miss Maude Russell clasped hands to her breasts.

None of them would have mentioned that Poppa McCall had been standing by with a shotgun if that elopement hadn't taken place. The upshot of it stood right across the room, the premature baby who had weighed eight pounds. She was shooing some grandkids now.

"What I remember, Tate, boy, was you singing 'The World Is Waiting for the Sunrise' at Miss Betty Crowley's funeral. You set this community on its ear."

"How come that?" a younger person asked.

"It wasn't church music," was the reply.

Half-grinning, Tate didn't mention that had been Miss Betty's request. He could see himself on that altar singing, " . . . sunrise!" while watching Dr. Crowley eye the woman who would be his next wife. He recalled again running through that September heat, the *whoosh* of knickers, the smell of carnations that would remind him of death even years later, and appearing in the man's kitchen shouting, "It's Poppa!" with that rattletrap trip home afterward. So that eyeing the man eyeing the woman at that funeral he had to forgive the doctor, because wasn't that what life was all about, some kind of trade-off? It seemed he had figured that out even as a younger man.

He no longer sang anything, even in silence. The world is wait-ting! The words rose up in his throat unheralded and hung there, cracking. That was my finest, my shining hour, he thought, singing a song at a funeral that nobody had ever heard sung at one before. And it wasn't even my idea.

Church music today could be a drumbeat, a xylophone, a horn tooting, a guitar, whatever the preacher, being young himself, brought in to woo young folks. Having his preacher running through town in jogging shorts went against Tate's grain; seeing the man's pale, thin legs bared like lily stalks gave him the sensation of seeing something he ought not, like the preacher's wife undressing, or the preacher peeing.

Brother Lott brought in youth groups to sing loud songs that were nothing but the same line repeated over . . . and over . . . and over. The man had people he called folksingers there on the altar singing way up in their noses and plucking and strumming chords on a guitar without ever really making music. Old folks in their pews stared at one another, and nothing they could do about it. Tate liked old-timey ways better, with the preacher shouting you were going to hell in a bucket if you didn't believe the Bible and making a sermon out of that. Brother Lott read poetry to them out of books, as if he couldn't think up anything of his own.

Tate finally had to escape the chair and the people, and unloosening his tie a bit, he wandered off. He passed young men talking about the need for a new fire truck. Not one of them thought about asking his advice or pulling him into the conversation. He wanted to say, I was one of the first volunteers!

They were talking about holding concerts here in the Community Center to raise money. Elvis impersonators; hard rock; heavy metal. Tate wasn't sure he knew what they were talking about. How about a cakewalk? he wanted to venture. *That's how we raised money in the first place.*

He set one foot in front of the other going in the dizzying, crazy pattern that was a cakewalk's. One of the young men grabbed his elbow, steadying, and said, "You all right, Mr. Tate?"

He told him, "Yes sir," and the boy let loose. "Mighty fine party," he told Tate, lying through his teeth, standing there drinking the sweet stuff, eating a teeny sandwich. He guessed the boy didn't know any other conversation to make.

" . . . fifty years later," the boy concluded, and Tate tried to fill in what he hadn't heard. Balloons outside were still popping. The young fellows stared at him as if he was something the cat dragged in. Imagine, they must be thinking, being married longer than other folks had been living.

"You're mighty nice to come," he told them, out of common courtesy. Behind his back, thinking Tate was out of earshot, one of the young men snickered, "Where would we rather be? Over on the dam water-skiing. Why, forget it." The rest of them laughed like a pack of jackals.

Tate kept on his same direction, a little dizzily. It overcame him sometimes in the bank or post office, and folks had to help him sit down while he took a nitroglycerin tablet. The doctor told Allie, "He can't go on being a menace to himself and others on the road." They were talking about country roads; he'd long since given up driving on highways.

"Tate. Had anything to eat?" Maude Russell propelled him along in her wake. "The food's so pretty." The food table was at the opposite end of the room, and near it he saw Allie stand up. Something was afoot.

Something he was going to have to take part in. In the kitchen, partly partitioned by a curtain, the cateress and her helper were busy. Tate saw them pull slices of white bread out of a polka-dot wrapper and cut holes in their middles with a juice glass.

Later, the cateress brushed the crusts into a garbage sack. Whoa there; wait a minute, he wanted to shout. How many bread puddings had he eaten from just such scraps back yonder when nobody wasted anything, in the Depression? Leftovers from leftovers went to hogs, and he'd carried out many a slop bucket. His eye caught that of the cateress, there in the kitchen with her shiny-armed helper. He'd eyed Esther Jones as long as he could remember, since the beginning, and he stood there singing silently words in his throat. He thought back to the first Sunday school class of all, the Cradle Roll, and eyeing Esther then, who must have known it too, because he had been a good-looking boy. Years later when he met her in the halls of whatever school, she'd given him special treatment, a lipsticky grin, a toothpasty smile, wiggling her hips. He stood now thinking about lost opportunities.

Try as he might, even then he had not been able to rid himself of Allie in his mind's eye. Their families must have always shoved them together, and there was not a time he could think of, even back to Cradle Roll, when he hadn't known he was going to marry Allie Gates.

If he'd been different, Tate thought, something might have happened with Esther instead of the nothing that took place. Eyes twinkling, he chose to look at her again—across that long space of years—but also across the distance from where he stood to the kitchen. Esther came out, wiping her face, and rounded the table. Uh oh, Tate told himself. Here came a big, three-tiered wedding cake being wheeled out, its icing thick and white. This was what all the ushering was about, the wake of the ladies and Allie crossing the room. "The photographer from *The Democrat*'s finally here," someone shouted.

Esther asked, "You got something in your eye, Tate?" She had brought him a dish towel with one wet end. He with a twinkle in his eye suddenly had a cast. Tate shook his head. You don't remember? he wanted to ask. He needed to get out of the place. Show the seat of, the dust of, his pants.

"I saw you looking like you had something in your eye," Esther said, straightening a tray of round sandwiches: white cut-outs sprinkled with paprika.

"Now who invited him?" Allie said.

To Tate's joy, Preacher Allan walked in. "We did, Aunt Allie," Ruthie said. "He's Uncle Tate's best friend."

"I know he is. I don't mind. I was just surprised," Allie said.

Hat in hand, Preacher moved toward the honored guests. Most of the people knew him, yet he could not help but duck his gray head, shy about being the only colored person present. "I'm glad you came," Tate said, shaking hands.

Preacher took the cup of punch offered, and Tate could not warn him in front of others. "I see you got trouble with your tractor," Preacher said.

Tate hung his head. He couldn't tell Preacher about the promise to himself. He said, "I didn't get finished cutting my grass."

"I'll come over tomorrow and he'p you," Preacher said.

"I don't know if I'm going to be here tomorrow or not, Preacher," Tate said. "I'll let you know if I am."

"Cake," people started crying, and they swarmed forward. The hefty young photographer apologized for being late. "We can start the cutting ceremony," a guest said. Tate froze. Had he heard right? He prayed not, but knew he was lost. Step up, fellow, he told himself. This many years later he would have to feel like a fool again. He would have to repeat what he had hated doing in the first place.

Here came the same silver cake knife gussied up with a bow ribbon. His and Allie's hands went atop one another. They would cut a slice, feed each other, nibble it up. The photographer would click, and tomorrow they'd show up in the paper with mouths full of cake. More cake than teeth, Tate thought. If the fool woman told him to smile for the birdie, he would leave.

"Smile for the birdie," the photographer said.

"Tate. What on this earth? You missed my mouth."

Young men guffawed. Tate's fingers were dabbled with icing, but Allie had it smeared by one ear. Grin for the camera, he remembered. *Grin grin grin.*

"Smile for the birdie," the photographer said again. Tate was being force-fed like a goose, gall and cake stuck in his gullet. Or maybe it was his heart.

Preacher delicately ate the second slice of cake that was cut, off a paper plate printed with wedding bells and two gold names. The nieces took over the cutting. Tate was free to wander after Preacher Allan when he left. He thanked the man a second time for coming; he wouldn't have wanted to be the only white man in a room full of colored. It was only recently the colors started inviting each other to events. Though white people had always gone where they wanted. How many colored churches had he sat outside of, listening to the singing, thinking when black people came out to pass the hat that they were just glad of the money? Maybe they had all along been full of resentment and hate that they couldn't say, Get out of my churchyard, white folks. How many colored friends had he gone to see buried, too, and been ushered to the front pew, an honored guest, sitting there with his neck prickling and glad to think, I'm white.

Preacher Allan would see him put six feet under, Tate felt. On the road the man clapped on his hat, and inside Tate watched him. "Come on," people called out. "The flowers are here." They were late arriving because the photographer kindly brought them from the Nashtoba florist. Clucking ladies dabbed icing from Allie's hair with paper napkins. Tate approached, and she told him, "Tate. I swear."

He and she stood together opening two waxy white boxes. Inside, in a lot of paper, they found flowers. Tate could not pin on Allie's so someone else stuck on her yellow orchid with tigerish brown spots. Tate stood still as a statue, eyes wandering, while Allie pinned to his lapel a perfect, pink-white rosebud reminding him of a baby's death.

Allie was tired and had to sit down. He bent over her. "Orchids don't smell, Tate," she said.

He drew back, taking his kiss with him, and told her, "You could wear that corsage to a ball game."

"Why, boy. Hush your mouth," she said. Allie never had had enough sense of humor to suit him, Tate thought.

She sat in an honorary chair, a yellow balloon tied to it denoting that. When he bent toward her, Tate spied an extra pin in her flower box, and since nobody seemed to be looking, he popped the balloon behind her.

Allie rose out of her chair, screaming. He saw then there could be consequences. She could break her old hip, she could break the new one. Allie grabbed hold of the heirloom lace tablecloth, borrowed for the day, that was covering the punch table. Ruthie, ladling punch, slopped it all over. Cups already filled spilled down the cloth to the floor, creating a lovely, yellow, puddling mess—little boys ran there like quicksilver to skate, slip, and slide in it. Parents ran after them to haul them back by their coattails, blaming each other that their children behaved so badly. Spats started. Little girls ran shrieking to avoid evil little boys with sticky yellow fingers and snarling teeth.

People started wiping at the floor with napkins, paper towels, and smelly dishrags from the kitchen. Esther and the helper ran in and out taking away dirty cups, bringing clean ones. The tablecloth's owner shook her head, frowning, saying, "It doesn't matter."

"Don't let anything else happen," Allie said. "Look at me. I'm ruint."

The front of her suit was covered with lemony, gummy drops. Tate stole off. A little girl's hand found its way into his. "Can I pop one?" she whispered.

They headed for the food table. On the way they stopped by a side table where a lot of the faceless, yellow, bald-headed fellows rose out of the flowers. Kneeling on a chair, the child could reach them.

Men were startled. The popping sounded like backfire on the road, or like gunshots, and hunting season hadn't even started. Mothers shook little boys who bawled their innocence. In all the commotion, the fugitives went about freely, popping balloons. Everybody thought heat caused the problem; the air-conditioners weren't adequate for the crowd. Now the heat was worse because people were leaving, and the door opening.

The sodden tablecloth had to be taken off. An ugly, plain, raw pine board lay underneath, over sawhorses that were just as bad, as basic and pitiful as any pauper's casket. "Watch out for splinters," a man said; but nobody was having any more punch: Thank you.

There was nothing to do but mop. Esther and her helper brought in a sudsy bucket of water and dipped and wrung till the place stank of disinfectant. Afterwards there were wide, wet places on the floor that old folks had to be skittish about. They held onto one another and headed for the door. Now Allie's eyes looked like wild violets with dew on them.

"Try you one of these sandwiches," the little girl told Tate. "They're awful."

He picked up a round hole of bread, watching as her braces turned red with paprika. She put what was left of her sandwich on the tray, a quarter-moon slice of bread with crimped edges from having been bitten. Tate bit into one in the same way, prepared to tell her it was only cucumber. But that was not the case. Beneath was something strange, strong, and fishy. He put his own quarter-moon back where he got it, on the ornate silver tray borrowed for the occasion.

The little girl's mother came over. "What were you talking to Mr. Tate about?" she asked.

"I asked why he did this," said the child, waggling her chin up and down in perfect imitation of a cow chewing or of Allie mocking him. Tate knew he never was going to remember where he hid those teeth from himself.

"I don't believe it's ruint," Allie said, looking at the tablecloth's owner, but with a question in her voice.

At the other end of the room, a man hollered, "A mouse has been nibbling the food."

"Only nibbling?" a man chortled. "Maybe that mouse don't like anchovy paste either."

Esther and the helper ran from the kitchen. Esther in horror stood crying, "There's no more bread." What did that matter, somebody asked. Nobody wanted more food. A small crowd of people shoved to the door. Ladies told Allie, "This party has been just lovely," as if not a thing in the world had occurred out of the ordinary.

Tate slipped out. On the road he stood impressed by the number of people who had come. He wondered who they all were and where they were going, feeling everybody but himself was busy. Nobody would miss this half of the honored guests leaving, he thought.

The tractor on its hillside loomed down at him. He went around to the shed. After all these years he knew still where an extra key to the truck stayed hidden. He rummaged behind hanging yellow slickers and orderly rows of boots. He set a fireman's hat on his head and groaned trying to swing up to the running board, first with one stiff leg and then with the other. Finally he dragged a stool over and made his way up. After a time he pulled himself onto the seat, knees first, his hands splayed like a child's learning to crawl. He sat up, squinting, and fumblingly inserted the key. Look out! he warned everyone in silence. The engine rumbled under him. With stiff fingers, his knuckles aching, he managed to start the siren. The fire truck rushed out into the clear, shining path always left open for it.

Cars pulled hurriedly to the side of the road. Customers ran out of Loma's old store at the truck's blaring. Partygoers stood stunned on the road. They called back to people inside, "It's Tate . . . Tate McCall running off!"

That was the last he saw or heard of them. The wind whipped in his direction. His hat tilted, and he righted it. He drove with the freedom of one hand. He turned down the sharp, steep road that led to the government dam. Nothing was beyond the road's end but the roaring, rushing water that was the dam's spillway, and a favorite spot for fishing. Beyond was the calm, opaque, muddy Mississippi water that was Itna Homa Lake. Only in the sun's right glance did it ever shine.

Tate had thoughtfully provided for himself. His pockets were crammed with mints emblazoned 50. He fingered them securely while the siren roared. People ran out of houses all along the way, sheltering their faces to the sun and staring. People tending gardens stood up out of them, like stalks. Kids on bikes rode faster, waving to the old man in the truck. If they missed the mints Tate threw, they got off their bikes to find them. There were black kids and white ones. All along the way people were doing what Sunday afternoon called for, napping under trees, cutting grass, visiting with the preacher.

Tate swept past, throwing mints. People ran out, gathering them up. He passed a small general store that stayed alive mostly by selling crickets for fishing. The crickets were out in the sun, chirping in bait boxes. The store's owner was an old woman he knew, Miss Annie. She came out to her one flat step, eyeglasses glinting. Tate tossed mints, which she caught in her apron, billowed out like a cloud. One time in her store she gave him a hunk of rat-trap cheese for tasting, so much he carried most of it home to Allie. All for nothing, for free! He tossed Miss Annie more mints going by.

As a kid he had gone to the Christmas parade in Memphis. People rode by on floats in tulle and velvet britches, society folks, he reckoned, tossing down candy. To common folks, he supposed, like me: faceless people in the dark standing on curbs.

Along the way people shouted at him, but Tate could not hear anything they said. Maybe they were trying to tell him the road ahead was dead end, as if he didn't know that, having lived here all his life. Soon there would be nothing but a ramp where people put in boats for fishing or sailing, and a large sign reading "Government Property."

It was much easier than Tate expected. He drove straight down past the sign and into the water. When his head went under, he heard the siren drown out, sputter, pop, like a spark plug's going, electricity shorting, or a firecracker's sizzling to its end. . . .

He came up and found himself standing on the truck's seat. This is not what I intended, Lord, he told himself. Even now, Tate could not shout. His lips seemed sealed, pasted together by the muddy water he could taste. The truck had gone so far out and could go no farther. There was a long way before the water grew deep. People were coming toward him—he began counting cars—one, two, and three. . . . Kids on bicycles pedaled faster toward him, shouting. No matter that he could have drowned, they cried, "Hooray!" Imagine the stories they'd have to tell in school on Monday.

Now people would watch him like a hawk. They would expect behavior that was wilder, stranger, crazier; he was certainly nutty as a fruitcake. They would jerk their kids out of his sight, his path, and his reach. It's worse, Tate thought. *It's worse than it ever has been in this world.*

He would be nothing but a doddering old fool, the town character, the town jerk—a loony. Maybe he ought to be put away in the asylum at Whitfield. Sweet, mild-mannered, passive Mr. Tate—what could have happened? It showed anybody at all could go off his rocker. People would start saying they had never known really what was inside him. It was often, you know, the sweetest, quietest ones you had to watch. They would warn Allie not to go to sleep beside him at night. He might turn murderous next.

Kids, having pedaled up, shied away when they reached the water. They only stood back and stared. Miss Annie at the store kept blinking, still holding up her apron, not knowing what she expected, but expecting something. Black people with fishing poles lashed to their cars like hoops rode toward him. Strange white boys looked at him from a battered car, laughing and smoking cigarettes. "Man," one of them said enviously, blowing acrid, scented smoke, "what a trip."

A flock of folks came running, walking, pedaling, driving toward him. And there's nothing I can do about it, Tate told himself. He could not even drown in his sorrow. He continued standing, his feet half-submerged, waiting and watching. Allie came finally in a long line of cars from the Center. She got out, tapping her cane toward the cobblestone ramp, helped along by nieces and nephews. Some of the nephews ran alongside, young fellows hollering about their fire truck and the damage to it. Would insurance cover this? Hey, fellow. It's your fault! You're guilty.

Suppose that sometime, tonight, tomorrow, next week, the entire community burned down, acres of it, waiting for a fire truck to come from the station in Whitehill, ten miles away? The nieces and nephews held Allie by the shoulders to steady her walk. Tapping on, she reached the water's edge to cry at last, "Tate. What on this earth?"

Her eyes too held that look of wonder, fear, distrust about a man without enough oxygen to his brain, which was not his case and never had been. . . .

Allie stood with her feet at the water's edge while gentle waves lapped back and forth, propelled by distant boats rushing toward where a fire truck was in the water. She tapped her cane one more time, asking again with all that support behind her, "Tate. What on this earth?"

He stared back in silence, saying, Happy anniversary.

NONFICTION

Seymour Lawrence Publisher

Years ago in Mississippi, William Faulkner read one of my first short stories and sent it away to his agent. Shortly, I received warm, complimentary letters from a young editor at *The Atlantic Monthly*—Seymour Lawrence—who accepted "The Morning and the Evening" as an *Atlantic* "First." We decided to meet in New York, where I was living, when he came to town—Faulkner would be there too, for lunch at the Harvard Club. He opened up to the tall, thin, shy young editor with a stutter, and reminisced at length about Sherwood Anderson. With the astuteness that would eventually make him a great publisher, the young editor said, "Why don't you write all that down for *The Atlantic*, Mr. Faulkner?"—which produced a long, beautiful cover story in such a short time that the amazed agent Harold Ober asked, "What did you do, Mr. Lawrence?"

Who can answer how Sam does what he does? It is partly the sure, swift instinct of a bloodhound that enables him to sniff out talent, originality, and good literature. His life has been singularly dedicated. But a large part, too, of his success is purely and simply devotion to long hours at his desk, to tedious detail, to work. God bless him.

Celebration

We know he was a reticent man, a shy man, a man who talked so little, sometimes, he made uncomfortable other people around him. What would he think then of our celebration?

He was a man, however, who wanted to make a mark on the wall, to say Kilroy was here. A man who in the office of his editor at Random House, Saxe Commins, pointed to a shelf full of his books one day and said, "Not a bad legacy for a man to leave behind."

He believed about writing that it was the answer, the reason for it all, the one and only way on earth to say *No!* to death: the best, the strongest, the finest, the most enduring: "to make something that wasn't here before us," he told me, something that doesn't just move you but that will tear your living entrails, and to create characters who will stand up and cast their own shadows, like his Caddy, he said that time.

In 1952, he wrote to me about himself this way: "Once there was a man, he had got pretty white on top because he had lived a goodish length of time, and he probably believed that his heart had got a little grey-headed too, because he had used his heart without much stint or calculation, to believe in and seek for beauty and truth and passion and pity, but most of all, to believe, to not be afraid or shocked by anything: using his heart to make of him a better person. To be gentle and tender and compassionate."

Those were the ideals he lived by and to which he dedicated his life. He only didn't live long enough.

But what happens when no one listens to what has been a man's life's dedication? When no one cares about his work and the ideals he believes in? It is easy when one is famous to shun the limelight, dodge it, and make that almost a game. But it is another thing altogether to be left in the shade, for it to seem the shelf of books to go unread, be out of print, that their titles will be known only in card catalogue files. Then there rises up the torment, what's it all been for? What does it mean? All the dedication. And for a writer, the solitude.

That was essentially the state Faulkner was in when I met him. I remember one time his quiet look of inner dejection and despair—and I regret I can't remember what words led up to his saying, "With the mark I seem to be about to leave on this world." Meaning, at the time, he seemed not to be about to leave any mark at all. It was as if I could see inside him to sorrow as he contemplated death and an oblivion he did not want. But he was not a man to rage. Even in torment he was quiet. In despair, he was still that which he set out to be, both—tender and gentle.

But he was Faulkner even then and he knew it. He knew it always. He knew from the beginning and signed his earliest letters to me that way, Faulkner. He knew it when he was only a country person in Mississippi as much as he ever was one. Knew it when he was a tramp in Grand Central Station looking for a warm place to be. It was only that he had to worry through conflicting periods of hope and despair, through trials and errors, whether anyone else would ever know it too. I've read that early on he annoyed Eudora Welty by signing himself simply that way, Faulkner. Who does he think he is? She apparently raged.

Fate changed for him as we know, and maybe he did not. But in 1953 while writing a fable, he looked back over it all assessing himself:

"This is my last major, ambitious work," he wrote to me, "the stuff is still good but there is not much more of it. A little trash keeps coming up. I'm getting to the bottom of the barrel."

But he did finally have a perspective on what he had done. "I mean," he continued in his letter, "work apart from me, the work which I did, apart from what I am."

"And now I realize for the first time what an amazing gift I had: uneducated in every formal sense, without even very literate, much less literary companions, yet to have made the things I made. I don't know where it came from. I don't know why God or Gods or whatever it was, selected me to be the vessel. Believe me, this is not humility, false modesty. It is simply amazement. I wonder if you have ever had that thought about the country man whom you know as Bill Faulkner—What little connection there seems to be between them."

The man and his work seemed always part and parcel of the whole to me, so dearly did I love the same land, its people and their spirit. Once a woman in a hamlet in Mississippi said to me, "Why do I want to read Faulkner? I grew up knowing all that." The old men on the store porches round their checker sets could have told the same tales, the quiet ladies at their quilting table. But they could not put them all down into written words. They did not have the artistry, the art of the written word which we are here tonight to celebrate—as well as the man who was such a master at it.

The man and his tales of the countryside flowed together for me, but he went on trying to make them separate. He wanted to be only the man who lived, wrote the books, and died, and that was all anybody needed to know, he felt. Only that is not how things work. We don't care what he ate for breakfast or what he wore when he slept. We care though about the spirit of the man and the rage and despair he felt for man in his condition, which he wanted to tell us about.

This man, too, cared also for his fellow artists. He cared about young people wanting to follow the craft and once wanted to set up a colony for them himself. His advice to the young writer was that the most important thing was the being willing to work—willing and ready to sacrifice everything for it if you were so unfortunate that that was what the Gods demanded. Only, he said, if you were really willing and ready, they would not ask so much.

So that of course he would be happy for our celebration tonight. There are people here putting out all effort to celebrate talent, to bring it to fruition by creating the William Faulkner Center of Literature. All of us here have been privileged to know him by one name or another: some as Mr. Faulkner, or Mister Bill, or simply by the name he called himself, Faulkner: and there are a few of us still around who could say the best of all, Bill.

He loved the celebration of birthdays. Mine is the day after his and through all the years, he never forgot. A telegram always arrived:

"Many happy returns on your birthday and love."

So at midnight we'll raise our glasses and say the same:

"Happy Birthday, Mister Faulkner. Thank you for the legacy you left us."

Remembering

It might not be true and does not much matter. But I remember him as a boy with curly hair. Frankie, everyone called him then. Brightly in my mind's eye, however, I see him in places we shared. Conversations will not come back because there were few. To ponder these many years later why the boy who became the poet Frank Stanford remembered me is to wonder if our tendencies toward silence were a bond between us I did not realize existed. Nothing could have startled me more than that he dedicated work to me.

In the summer of 1964, I was thirty-five and still feeling my way as a writer: inwardly attuned and outwardly coping with being a wife, housekeeper, and the mother of two sons, then eight and nine. Even so young they were my buffers against the world. I travelled behind their lively personalities, keeping my solitude. That summer Frankie was fourteen. With my sons I visited for a month, doing research that became my second novel. In the household also were his sister Ruth, not blood-related, and their adoptive mother, Dorothy. The house was fashioned for informality and, perched at the end of a point of land called Mallard Point, in the Arkansas Ozarks, was surrounded on two sides by a lake. I remember my sons' disappointment at not being able to shoot their BB guns in what seemed country. The lake created activity, swimming, boating and water-skiing. My research consisted of scattered conversations with Dorothy Stanford, something important perhaps surfacing while we were drying dishes. I do not remember writing on my book at all, and the only typing was a book review for *Life* magazine. If I was Frankie's first introduction to a writer, it was not a fair picture. I was not behind closed doors often.

I asked my sons what they remember and they say, Mom! we were kids. Yet in their brief glimpses something is to be learned, for Frankie could well have ignored them as pests. They remember breaking his good guitar and that he didn't get mad, that he took them on his boat and taught them to fish, and that once he had them down on his bed hitting them with a pillow and, swinging it, broke the ceiling light. And that I remember: coming in from an adjoining bedroom at the sound of shattering glass. And I see him again still kneeling, pillow in hand, lightly smiling and afraid I've come angry because of his roughhousing. He had cut his arm, and my youngest son laughs, aping Frankie's thick Southern accent when he asked his sister for a Band-Aid and recalls the natural, healthy carping between them about who was going to get it.

Quiet: but I never once thought of him as an unhappy boy. He would look at me directly though shyly, and usually wearing a little smile that strikes me afterward too as containing something of uncertainty. Only now can I think the smile perhaps indicative that he was listening already to some other, interior self. My impression mostly was of a sturdy, muscular boy, busy with a summer job on the lake. Our memories are scanty because like any boy his age he was not around a lot. I do not recall books in the house, unless there were a few in shelves on either side of a stone fireplace in the large main room. And I do not recall books in Frankie's room. There was nothing to make me expect to receive poems one day with an inscription across the top: *You never knew I was in the next room writing too.*

Talk was not of writers or writing and no one knew I knew William Faulkner. It would not have occurred to me the boy Frankie would have been interested, or known who the man was, anyway. And it did not occur to me unhappiness would strike us all too soon.

My boys' father came for a short visit. His memory? Frankie met him almost at the front door with a box of elaborate fishing tackle, asking questions Mr. Bowen could not answer. He sensed disappointment, felt Frankie veer off, and does not remember any contact afterward. Ezra was then an editor of *Sports Illustrated*, and I feel Frankie had an idealized vision not only of a New York editor but particularly one from a sports magazine, being so physical himself. I knew Frankie was adopted, but perhaps Ezra did not know the similarity in their backgrounds. His parents divorced when he was three and his father never saw him again and died when Ezra was eighteen. I had seen the toll that blankness took. And much older, Frankie would think of moving to New York and ask if he could contact Mr. Bowen: whether to ask for a job, or merely about the city I don't know. But I remember being glad that Frankie never made the move, glad he wisely stayed with what he did know had formed him: that land, those mountains, and the people he had known always.

I was a teen-ager when I first heard about a baby named Frank Stanford. I never asked Dorothy until after his death if Frankie knew he was adopted. She had thought he had always known: had made it clear from the beginning that he was a chosen child, and grafted into her family from the minute he was born. Then, unexpectedly, he came home in high school one day and asked if she'd adopted him. And after that, she said, he never seemed the same again.

The man for whom he was named, the only father he ever knew, was an older friend of my father's. He was called 'Mister Frank' by even his peers, out of respect. When he came to our house I was impressed by this tall, spare, silver-haired and soft-spoken gentleman. He was the only friend my father had who I knew had been to college. An engineer, Mister Frank helped build the levee system along the Mississippi River in the Mid-South as we know it today. My father sold him dynamite and did blasting for him. My second novel was to be about my father, and I had come to Dorothy for information about those days. Levee camps were tough places, and people in them rough. Mister Frank seemed the antithesis of his working world. Heat was nearly tropical, and there were tents to live in, mosquitoes, poisonous snakes, and a few white faces among many black ones. Into this environment

Frankie came as a baby. After his first wife's death, Mister Frank married Dorothy, who already had her two adopted babies, unusual for a single woman in that time. Not many women could have endured camp life the way she did, loved it even. But in the wintertime the Stanfords lived in a fine house in Memphis.

My first memory of Dorothy and of Frankie was when he was nine or ten. The levee camp days were over; my father was dead; I was visiting in Memphis with thoughts of my novel vague. One evening I went to a Little League game with the Stanfords, and Frankie hit his first home run! Afterward we gathered about him excitedly, and I see that half-smile on the face of a tired, dusty boy, pleased with himself. Dorothy was such a warm, loving person that that evening she brought me to tears. Simply, she suffused me with a sense of caring that I had missed in my childhood and looked for still. There was the same age difference between us as between Frankie and me. Gossip had reached my teen-age ears, and I knew she gave Mister Frank a love and warmth he had not had before, either. My voice broke when I tried to congratulate him on having her. 'Dorothy affects everyone that way,' he said in his quiet manner. 'She is a wonderful woman.'

Next I see them all at Mallard Point, on an overnight visit, after Mister Frank has retired there. In that memory Frankie is truly only a boy in the background, coming and going. Not only is Mister Frank old but ill, walking with one foot shuffling ahead of the other, listing slightly backward, and leaning totally for support on Dorothy. She nursed him with wonderful patience. Yet I could feel glad for them, because their love and respect for one another was something to be envied. It was that example Frankie had before him, growing up in a house without strife. I did think, though, about my boys and their relationship with their father, and how hard it was for the boy there to have a father not only so old but dying before his eyes.

By the time of my long visit, the next summer, Frankie is the man in the household. Only Mr. Bowen's brief visit gave him respite from taking us out on the boat when anyone wanted to go. One afternoon Mr. Bowen pulled up to a pier and Frankie appeared to pump our gas. The boys and I exclaimed in surprise: meaning, here's where Frankie disappears to everyday! I recall him as saying nothing but wearing his same slight smile, perhaps saying a great deal, but seeming only pleased too by our surprise, and discovery.

In back, there was a patio where Dorothy and I often sat alone in the evenings, watching stars and a light that circled at regular intervals. Those who lived there and saw it regularly claimed it was a UFO. It was a pleasant time for the adults, when everyone was fed and the house settled. On a wall in my house now there is a picture taken on that patio. Two small brothers have their arms about one another and are smiling and holding up fishing rods. Behind them the lake is so intensely blue it seems to be dancing, despite having been stilled permanently in the sunlight by the camera. Ill winds had not yet blown in to touch us. The little boys had no idea that within a few years their parents would divorce rather unthinkingly: lives gone atilt would never right themselves in the same way again. Nothing told us of Frankie's incipient genius, or that tragedy lay ahead for those who knew him. For is it tragedy for him if he chooses to leave us? Those closest knew, afterward, the times he was saying so painstakingly goodbye.

After Mallard Point I saw him only once again, in the early 1970's. Re-married, I was living on a plantation in Mississippi. With his wife Ginny and a friend, Frankie came to interview me while doing a documentary on women writers. He was striking in a white suit and a panama hat, and when he came in I thought that I shouldn't call him Frankie anymore. When my oldest son came downstairs Frankie said, Why, I can't get over Ezra! And I laughed and told him that was the same way I felt about seeing him after so many years.

Then it was hot October and intermittently there were shots in the milky air, and a dove hunt was going on nearby. The interview took place outdoors and the visitors could not stay afterward. Ginny and the friend went ahead, and Frankie purposefully lingered so that we were alone. Perhaps in that lingering there was some attempt to recapture that other time, when Mister Frank was alive, and my father, and there were dynamiting days on the levee. He wanted to go and find all the old levee people he could, black and white, and capture their memories on tape before they were gone, and promised to take me with him. Then without prompting he began to tell me how happy he was! That with Ginny he had the relationship with a woman he'd longed for. And I see him moving about as if he needed exertion to tell me the final summation about his life: everything was going well and far better than he could ever have dreamed. When he left I was filled with so much happiness, thinking how far he had come.

I cannot remember whether I heard from him again. But a few years later I was living in Connecticut and opened a letter from Ginny which explained about his death, and enclosed an obituary. Long afterward Dorothy would cry in her mother's anguish, Oh, didn't he know when he killed himself he killed me too!

My God: Frankie, I thought: and felt so much guilt. Had he, in sending me poems and a short story over the years, been asking something which I in my replies did not give? It is a natural reaction to someone's suicide to think, Where did I fail? What could I have done? Though, finally, absolving myself of guilt, and no longer even asking why, I only hope Frank found what he wanted. And maybe that was not even peace, but who he was. At last.

Acknowledgments

A special note of gratitude for my husband, Jess Bunn, whose unflagging encouragement, support, and editorial assistance enhance this book and all my other efforts. And for my additional editorial wonders—Susannah Northart, James Roper, and Karen Wright—all writers should be blessed with such keenly attentive and talented readers. Susannah, thank you for the second go-round!

My enduring appreciation to family and friends—for their affection and interest—especially my mother, an early and passionate women's advocate. To Jeffrey Michael Bunn and Jordan Arch Wilson—we are fortunate parents of a son and daughter who continue to surprise with their insight and grace. And to James, missed as much today as ever.

As always, an enthusiastic thank you to Sandy Baldwin for the talent and dedication she devotes to ballet and our ballet classes.

Thank you to the individuals who helped me with the research required to locate some of these more obscure pieces: Head of Archives and Special Collections at the University of Mississippi, Jennifer Ford; Former Head of Archives and Special Collections at the University of Mississippi, Thomas Verich; and Memphis rare book dealer, Susan Davis. To the editors of the publications where Joan Williams' fiction and nonfiction originally appeared, thank you so much for your cooperation!

To the estate of Joan Williams, her literary executor and son, Matthew Bowen, and her son, Ezra Bowen. Thank you to Seymour Lawrence's daughter, Macy Lawrence Ratliff. I also appreciate the assistance of Jeanne Byington of JM Byington & Associates, Inc.; Craig Tenney at Harold Ober Associates; David Adams, Michael Palgon, and Laura Tomenendal at Open Road.

And a particular thank you to Leonard Gill who acquainted me with Open Road's recognition and revival of Joan Williams' oeuvre.

I envisioned such a book over the many years of my friendship and interviews with Joan. Thank you all for helping me realize *Remembering*.